PENGUIN BOC

Vegetarian

BIBLE

Vegetarian
BIBLE

Margaret Barca

Contents

Introduction

Vegetarian food isn't — or shouldn't be — dull and boring. It should be adventurous and satisfying, a way of enjoying fresh and natural produce — from fruits and vegetables, pulses and grains to nuts and seeds, and in many cases, dairy products. A vegetarian meal can be rustic and robust, or as light and elegant as any fine-dining fare. It's not about what you *don't* eat (meat and seafood) — it's all about the fantastic healthy food you *can* eat and enjoy.

It doesn't matter why you have chosen not to eat meat (for ethical, health or perhaps religious reasons), or whether you're a full-time vegetarian, a vegan, or someone who just likes eating the occasional meal without meat, you will find recipes here that call on cultures from around the world, that use wonderful fresh ingredients, that look good, taste good and *are* good for you.

Basics

What is a vegetarian?

There are different 'types' of vegetarians. Most people think of a vegetarian as someone who eats no meat, but strictly speaking, a vegetarian also eats no dairy foods or seafood. Most Australians who are vegetarians are lacto-ovo vegetarians, which means they eat dairy products (such as cheese and yoghurt) as well as eggs.

Then there are 'part-time' or 'semi' vegetarians, who usually do not eat red meat but may occasionally eat seafood, or even white meat such as chicken.

What is a vegan?

Vegans eat no animal products at all, i.e. no meat, poultry, seafood, dairy foods, eggs, honey, gelatine or other animal by-products. They need to be more cautious than lacto-ovo vegetarians to ensure they are getting enough protein and nutrients. For that reason, vegans are often very conscious

of dietary requirements and make positive choices to ensure a healthy diet.

Protein

People who start eating a vegetarian diet are sometimes concerned about where they will get their protein. For those who eat dairy products and eggs, it is not too difficult as these foods are high in protein.

However, for longer-term health, you do need to re-think your diet, rather than just stop eating meat. If you have been eating meat and decide to eat less of it, it is important not to go from 'meat and three veg' to just 'three veg'. A balanced vegetarian diet is all about the range and variety of foods you consume, as well as their freshness and the fact that they are natural and unprocessed. Grains, pulses, nuts and seeds, as well as fruit and vegetables (and dairy foods for some) create a diet that is nutritionally rich and varied.

Non-animal foods can not provide complete protein if eaten individually, but when combined they can provide the protein needed. Pulses eaten at the same time as grains, nuts and seeds do form complete protein. So, think felafel with wholemeal bread and hummus (thus combining chickpeas, wheat and sesame seeds); or tofu with buckwheat noodles (soybeans with buckwheat and wheat); or even baked beans on toast. In fact, nutritionists now believe that these foods can be combined in the course of a day, not necessarily in one meal.

To increase the variety of foods you eat, it's also important to look beyond the standard pulses and grains. Try eating different types of pulses, such as black-eyed beans or chickpeas. Instead of wheat bread, try wholegrain rye or corn bread. Instead of white rice, try wild rice, polenta or buckwheat.

You can also add seeds and nuts to your diet: snack on sunflower seeds or mixed nuts; add a sprinkling of seeds or nuts to a salad. Buy raw, unsalted nuts and if you want to, lightly toast them just before eating. Buy nuts in small quantities and store them in a sealed container in a cool place.

Carbohydrates and fibre

A healthy, well-balanced vegetarian diet will be high in complex carbohydrates, including foods such as lentils, beans, grains, potatoes and bananas. Carbohydrates tend to get a bad rap these days, but these complex carbohydrates are filling and provide slow-release energy; it is the fats people tend to eat with them that are more likely to be fattening. For those who are not used to eating a high-carbohydrate and naturally high-fibre diet, it is worth introducing these foods relatively slowly at first until the digestive system becomes used to them. This is especially the case with younger children, particularly if they have previously been eating highly refined foods.

Fruit and vegetables are important providers of fibre (as well as myriad vitamins and nutrients), so it's important to eat plenty of them. Experiment and try different varieties. Look for really fresh organic food that is in season.

What about iron and calcium?

Lacto-ovo vegetarians can usually get enough iron and calcium from cheeses, yoghurt and eggs, as well as pulses, grains, vegetables and so on. For those who avoid dairy products and eggs, more emphasis needs to be put on eating wholemeal bread, dried fruits (such as figs), nuts (especially almonds and brazil nuts), soybean products (such as fortified soy milk and tofu), and parsley and dark-green leafy vegetables to ensure adequate iron and calcium. (Those who are concerned with their levels of iron and calcium should check with their medical practitioner.)

Vitamin B12

Those who eat dairy products and eggs should not have to worry about their B12 levels, but it is harder for vegans to obtain this vitamin from their diet. Mushrooms, tofu and fortified soy milk are all sources, though some people do take a vitamin B12 supplement. If you are concerned, check with you medical practitioner.

Vegan recipes

Many of the recipes in this book are suitable for vegans, or can be made to be with a very minor adaptation (for example, by using soy yoghurt instead of cow's milk yoghurt.) A note at the end of each recipe lets you know if the dish is vegan, or which ingredients can be substituted or omitted to make it vegan.

Soups

Soups are a fantastic, easy way to consume loads of vegetables, beans, grains and herbs, all in one bowl. With a leafy salad and some crusty bread, soup can be the heart of a healthy mid-week meal, or a fuss-free way to cater for friends.

Adding extra flavour and nourishing goodness is simple: add some beans or rice to a vegetable soup or stir in a spoonful of pesto; dollop some yoghurt into a spicy soup; or sprinkle some multigrain croutons over a creamy soup.

Excellent soups can be made using water, but a good vegetable stock will definitely add depth of flavour. If you use a ready-made rather than a homemade stock, start by using half stock and half water, as the commercial products can be very salty.

‹ Basic vegetable stock (page 12)

Basic vegetable stock

3 tablespoons olive oil

1 large brown onion, diced

2 medium-sized leeks, sliced

2 stalks celery (and some leaves
   if you have them), sliced

2 large carrots, peeled
   and sliced

3 cloves garlic, peeled

8 sprigs fresh parsley

3 sprigs fresh thyme

1 bay leaf

6 peppercorns

1 teaspoon salt

4 litres water

Heat oil in a stockpot over medium heat. Add onion, leeks, celery, carrots
and garlic, and sauté, stirring, for about 5 minutes. Add parsley, thyme, bay
leaf, peppercorns, salt and water and bring to the boil. Skim any scum from
the surface and simmer, uncovered, for 1–2 hours.

Strain stock and refrigerate for 3–4 days, or freeze for up to 2 months.

You can also buy vegetable stock in liquid, powdered and cube form.
Check the ingredients to be sure what you are buying as some of
them have unnecessary additives. If you are really short of time you
can make a quick stock with water, soy sauce, pepper and fresh
herbs – just simmer for a few minutes, then use.

MAKES ABOUT 3 LITRES | VEGAN

Ginger miso noodle soup

225 g fresh or dried udon
   noodles

6 cups water

¼ cup tamari

½ cup thickly sliced fresh ginger

120 g firm organic tofu,
   cut into 2-cm cubes

2 spring onions, finely sliced

¼ cup white miso

1 tablespoon sesame oil

Place the udon noodles in plenty of boiling water and cook according to packet instructions, or until tender (fresh noodles cook much more quickly than dried ones). Drain, rinse under cold water, drain again and set aside.

To make the broth, place the water, tamari and fresh ginger in a saucepan and bring to the boil. Reduce heat and simmer for 10 minutes. Remove ginger with a slotted spoon. Gently stir in the tofu and half the spring onions. Reduce the heat to very low.

Place the white miso in a small bowl. Add some of the broth and stir to dilute the miso. Pour the miso mixture into the remaining broth, then stir in sesame oil and noodles. Heat gently for 1 minute (do not boil).

Use tongs to lift noodles into individual bowls. Pour in broth and sprinkle with remaining spring onions.   >

Udon are Japanese wheat noodles – they are white, thick, and mild in flavour; perfect in a broth. Miso is a highly nutritious fermented paste made from soybeans mixed with a grain, such as barley or rice – add it at the last minute and do not overheat or you will destroy the beneficial micro-organisms.

SERVES 4 | VEGAN

Honey & mustard pumpkin soup

1 tablespoon olive oil

1 onion, sliced

1½ teaspoons ground cumin

2.5 kg pumpkin, peeled and
cut into small chunks

7 cups vegetable stock

2 tablespoons honey

2 tablespoons Dijon mustard

salt and freshly ground
black pepper

natural yoghurt, to serve

extra ground cumin, to serve

Heat oil in a large saucepan over medium heat, add onion and sauté for 5 minutes or until soft. Add cumin and stir for 1 minute. Add pumpkin and stock, bring to the boil, then reduce heat to medium, cover and simmer for about 20 minutes, until pumpkin is soft. Stir in honey and mustard.

Leave soup to cool for a few minutes, then purée in batches in a blender or food processor. Return to the saucepan and gently reheat. The soup should be quite thick. If not, continue to cook until the soup thickens.

Serve with a dollop of yoghurt and a sprinkle of cumin.

SERVES 6 | VEGAN: OMIT YOGHURT OR SUBSTITUTE
WITH SOY YOGHURT

Indian-spiced red lentil soup

8–10 cardamom pods

2 tablespoons vegetable oil

2 onions, chopped

3 cloves garlic, sliced

2 teaspoons ground turmeric

pinch of ground chilli

1 tablespoon grated fresh ginger

2 cups red lentils, rinsed

6 cups vegetable stock

1 bay leaf

2–3 tablespoons fresh
lemon juice

salt and freshly ground
black pepper

naan bread, to serve

Place cardamom pods in a mortar and crush. Remove seeds and set aside; discard pods.

Heat oil in a large saucepan over medium heat, add onion, cover and cook for 4–5 minutes until softened. Add cardamom seeds, garlic, turmeric, ground chilli and ginger and sauté, stirring, for 3–4 minutes.

Add lentils, stock and bay leaf and bring to the boil. Reduce heat and simmer, uncovered, for 20–25 minutes. Stir in lemon juice and season with salt and freshly ground pepper to taste.

Serve with warmed naan bread.

SERVES 4 | VEGAN

Minestrone

1 tablespoon olive oil

2 cloves garlic, crushed

1 onion, chopped

3 tablespoons roughly chopped
   flat-leaf parsley

2 large tomatoes, chopped

2 stalks celery, chopped

2 carrots, peeled and chopped

2 potatoes, peeled and chopped

5 cups vegetable stock

2 tablespoons tomato paste

1 zucchini, cut into thick slices

½ cup sliced green beans

¾ cup small pasta shapes

1 × 400-g can cannellini beans,
   drained and rinsed

salt and freshly ground
   black pepper

extra parsley and grated
   parmesan cheese, to serve

Heat oil in a large saucepan or stockpot over medium heat, add garlic and onion and sauté for 4–5 minutes until soft. Add parsley, tomatoes, celery, carrots, potatoes and stock, bring to the boil, then cover and simmer for 15 minutes.

Stir in tomato paste, zucchini, green beans and pasta shapes and simmer for a further 15 minutes. Add cannellini beans and cook for 5 minutes or until heated through, then season with salt and pepper.

To serve, sprinkle with finely chopped parsley and grated parmesan cheese.

SERVES 6

Moroccan tomato & chickpea soup

1 cup dried chickpeas
  (or 1 × 400-g can chickpeas,
  drained and rinsed)

1 cup brown lentils, rinsed

1 cinnamon stick

1 bay leaf

2 tablespoons olive oil

1 large brown onion, diced

2 cloves garlic, crushed

1 teaspoon ground cardamom

1 teaspoon ground coriander

5 cups vegetable stock

1 teaspoon salt

1 × 800-g can crushed tomatoes

2–3 tablespoons fresh
  lemon juice

salt and freshly ground
  black pepper

natural yoghurt, to serve

small fresh mint leaves, to serve

cayenne pepper, to serve

Place dried chickpeas in a bowl, cover with plenty of water and soak overnight. Drain and place in a large saucepan, then cover with plenty of fresh water. Bring to the boil, skim surface, then reduce heat, partially cover and simmer for 1 hour.

Add lentils, cinnamon stick and bay leaf and simmer for a further 30 minutes, or until chickpeas and lentils are tender. Drain and remove cinnamon stick and bay leaf. >

Heat oil in a large saucepan or stockpot over medium heat. Sauté onion, garlic, cardamom and coriander for about 5 minutes, until onion is softened. Add stock, salt and tomatoes. Bring to the boil, reduce heat and simmer for about 15 minutes.

Add chickpeas and lentils and simmer until just heated through. Add lemon juice, salt and freshly ground pepper to taste.

To serve, ladle into bowls, add a small dollop of yoghurt, a few small mint leaves and a sprinkle of cayenne pepper.

🍄 If you are using canned chickpeas, rinse well and add to the soup when you add the cooked lentils. This soup is even better then next day when the flavours have had time to develop.

SERVES 6 | VEGAN: SUBSTITUTE SOY YOGHURT FOR NATURAL YOGHURT

Pea & mint soup with fetta toasts

1 tablespoon olive oil

1 onion, diced

1 floury potato, diced

500 g shelled peas
(fresh or frozen)

7–8 fresh mint leaves

1 litre vegetable stock

½ cup milk (or ¼ cup cream
if preferred)

salt and freshly ground
black pepper

FETTA TOASTS

4 thick slices grainy bread

olive oil, for brushing

50 g soft fetta

freshly ground black pepper

Heat oil in a large saucepan, add onion and sauté over medium heat for 2–3 minutes, or until onion is transparent. Add potato, peas, mint and stock, stir well and simmer for 10–15 minutes. Purée in a blender or food processor until creamy. Return to the saucepan, stir in milk (or cream), season with salt and pepper and gently reheat (do not boil). If soup is too thick, add a little extra water or milk.

To make fetta toasts, lightly toast the bread, brush with olive oil and spread generously with fetta. Add a sprinkle of freshly ground black pepper and serve with the soup.

SERVES 4

Provincial bean soup with pesto

300 g flageolet beans

2 tablespoons olive oil

1 clove garlic, crushed

2 onions, chopped

250 g carrots, peeled and diced

1 leek, finely sliced

2 zucchinis, thickly sliced

2½ cups water or vegetable stock

salt and freshly ground
black pepper

3 tablespoons pesto (page 233)

Place beans in a bowl, cover with plenty of cold water and leave to soak for at least 6 hours, or overnight. Drain, place in a saucepan, cover with plenty of fresh water, bring to the boil and simmer for 1 hour, or until tender. Drain.

Heat oil in a large, heavy-based saucepan over medium heat, add garlic, onion and carrot and sauté, stirring, for 4–5 minutes. Add leek and cook for a further 4–5 minutes, until vegetables start to soften. Add zucchini, beans and water or stock. Bring to the boil and simmer for 10 minutes, or until vegetables are soft. Check for seasoning.

Ladle soup into warmed bowls, add a generous spoonful of pesto to each bowl and serve with plenty of crusty French bread. >

Flageolet beans are small white French beans. Use a 400-g can of beans if you prefer (rinse well and drain before adding), but note that these canned beans can be a bit mushy.

SERVES 6 | VEGAN

Ravioli in brodo
with asparagus & peas

6 asparagus spears, trimmed (see note on page 178)

6 cups vegetable stock

300 g cheese-filled ravioli

½ cup shelled peas (fresh or frozen)

2 tablespoons freshly grated parmesan cheese

Slice asparagus on an angle into 3-cm lengths. Heat vegetable stock and when boiling add ravioli, asparagus and peas. Return almost to boiling, then reduce heat to a simmer and cook for about 5 minutes. (Check cooking instructions for ravioli as cooking time varies and it is important not to overcook the pasta. Also, don't boil too vigorously or the pasta will split open.)

To serve, ladle into bowls and sprinkle with grated parmesan.

Tortellini in brodo is a classic Italian home-style dish: small, filled pasta in a tasty stock. This variation is more substantial, using slightly larger cheese-filled ravioli plus some vegetables. You can use other pastas with different fillings, but they shouldn't be too large. This is a great supper dish or easy Sunday night meal.

SERVES 4

Russian borscht

500 g beetroot

1 carrot, peeled and chopped

1 potato, peeled and quartered

1 leek, sliced

1 onion, quartered

¼ cup fresh lemon juice

½ teaspoon ground allspice

½ teaspoon ground nutmeg

1 tablespoon chopped fresh dill

2 bay leaves

6 cups vegetable stock

salt and freshly ground
  black pepper

natural yoghurt or sour cream,
  to serve

3 tablespoons chopped fresh
  dill, to serve

Wearing rubber gloves to avoid staining your fingers, wash, trim and peel beetroot and cut into chunks. Place beetroot, carrot, potato, leek, onion, lemon juice, spices, dill and bay leaves in a large saucepan with the stock. Bring to the boil, reduce the heat, partially cover and simmer for 2 hours, stirring occasionally.

Allow soup to cool a little, then blend in batches in a blender or food processor until smooth. Season with salt and freshly ground pepper to taste. Return to saucepan and gently reheat.

Serve with a small dollop of yoghurt or sour cream and a sprinkling of fresh dill.

SERVES 6 | VEGAN: OMIT YOGHURT OR SOUR CREAM,
OR SUBSTITUTE WITH SOY YOGHURT

Tomato soup with sesame stars

SESAME STARS

1 sheet ready-rolled puff pastry, defrosted

milk for brushing

2–3 tablespoons sesame seeds

SOUP

2 tablespoons olive oil

1 red onion, chopped

3 cloves garlic, chopped

1.5 kg vine-ripened tomatoes, chopped

5–6 fresh basil leaves, chopped

1 litre vegetable stock

1 cup milk

salt and freshly ground black pepper

2 tablespoons torn fresh basil leaves, to serve

Preheat oven to 200°C. Grease a baking tray.

To make sesame stars, use a star-shaped biscuit cutter to cut shapes from the puff pastry. Brush stars with milk, then press on enough sesame seeds to completely cover the top of each biscuit. Place onto the prepared tray and bake for 10–15 minutes, until golden. Place on a wire rack (you can serve these warm or cold).

To make tomato soup, heat oil in a saucepan, add onion and garlic and sauté for 2–3 minutes. Add tomatoes and basil leaves and cook until tomatoes start to soften and break down. Add stock and simmer for 25–30 minutes. >

Pour soup into a bowl and leave to cool a little, then blend in a food processor or blender. Pour through a sieve back into the saucepan. Add milk and reheat but do not boil. Check for seasoning.

Ladle into serving bowls and sprinkle with torn basil. Serve with sesame stars on the side.

🍄 Make this soup in summer when tomatoes and basil are at their very best.

SERVES 4 | VEGAN: SUBSTITUTE SOY MILK FOR MILK IN THE SOUP; SESAME STARS ARE NOT SUITABLE FOR VEGAN DIETS

Yellow split pea soup

500 g yellow split peas, rinsed

1 onion, chopped

1 bay leaf

9 cups vegetable stock

salt and freshly ground black pepper

extra virgin olive oil, to serve

1 tablespoon chopped fresh chives, to serve

Put the split peas, onion, bay leaf and stock in a heavy-based non-stick saucepan or medium-sized stockpot. Bring to the boil, skim any scum from the surface, reduce heat, partially cover and simmer for 50–60 minutes, stirring occasionally, until split peas are tender.

If the soup is too thick, add some extra water or stock while cooking. Season with salt and freshly ground pepper if needed.

Serve with a drizzle of olive oil, a sprinkle of chives and plenty of crusty bread on the side.

SERVES 4 | VEGAN

Eggs & cheese

High in protein, delicious and surprisingly versatile, both eggs and cheese can provide the foundation of many quick and easy non-meat meals. However, they can be high in fat and cholesterol, so think of them as complementary additions to a vegetarian or semi-vegetarian diet, rather than making them the basis of it.

Almost everyone can enjoy indulging in rich brie or gorgonzola — at least occasionally — but on a day-to-day basis, the ideal cheeses to look for are fresh, low-fat, soft or semi-soft cheeses such as ricotta, cottage cheese, mozzarella, fetta and haloumi. Swiss, tasty and parmesan cheeses are useful in moderate amounts. For vegans there are soy cheeses, though they can be quite expensive and are not to everyone's taste.

When buying eggs, look for free-range or organic. Check the use-by date and store them in the refrigerator.

< Baked ricotta (page 34)

Baked ricotta

500-g piece ricotta
2 tablespoons olive oil
salt and freshly ground black pepper

The ricotta should be fresh but not too moist. If it is very soft, line a sieve with a piece of clean muslin and place the sieve over a bowl. Carefully put ricotta in the sieve, cover and refrigerate for a few hours or overnight, to allow excess moisture to drain away.

Preheat oven to 220°C. Lightly grease a non-stick baking tray or dish with oil.

Place ricotta onto prepared tray, brush all over with olive oil and season with salt and freshly ground pepper. Bake for 25–30 minutes. Remove from oven and leave to cool.

🍴 Serve at room temperature with salad, or as part of an antipasto platter. The roasted red capsicum and walnut dip on page 235 or the black olive tapenade on page 223 go well with this dish.

SERVES 4–6

Frittata with spaghetti & herbs

5 eggs

½ cup grated parmesan cheese

½ cup milk

½ cup ricotta

salt and freshly ground
black pepper

200 g cooked thin spaghetti

2 tablespoons chopped
flat-leaf parsley

1 tablespoon chopped fresh
basil leaves

1 tablespoon olive oil

1 tablespoon butter

extra 2 tablespoons grated
parmesan cheese

1 heaped tablespoon pine nuts

Place eggs, parmesan, milk, ricotta, salt and freshly ground pepper in a large bowl and beat until just combined (it shouldn't be too frothy). Add cooked spaghetti and herbs and stir.

Heat oil and butter in a large non-stick frying pan over medium heat. Pour in frittata mixture, spreading pasta evenly over the pan and ensuring it is completely covered with the egg mixture. Reduce heat and cook for 7–8 minutes, occasionally lifting the sides a little to make sure it is not burning underneath.

While it is cooking, preheat grill to high. >

When frittata is almost cooked (there will still be some uncooked egg mix on top) sprinkle with the extra parmesan and pine nuts, and place under the grill for a few minutes. When parmesan and nuts are lightly browned, frittata should be cooked. It will continue to cook as it cools.

Serve the frittata just warm or at room temperature with a leafy salad.

SERVES 4

Grilled haloumi & asparagus

20 asparagus spears, trimmed (see note on page 178)

olive oil, for brushing

freshly ground black pepper

500 g haloumi, cut into thick slices

salsa verde with basil (page 236)

1 large lemon, cut into 8 wedges

Preheat barbecue or oven grill to high. Brush asparagus with oil and season with pepper. Barbecue or grill for 5–6 minutes, turning once or twice.

Place haloumi onto the barbecue or grill and cook for 2–3 minutes, turning once, until lightly browned and starting to melt. (If you prefer, cook the haloumi in a large non-stick frying pan that has been brushed with a little oil – it takes about the same time.)

Divide asparagus between four plates, top with grilled haloumi, spoon over salsa verde and place lemon wedges on the side. Serve immediately.

Haloumi cheese has a very high melting point, which makes it excellent for grilling or frying – you can get a lovely charred outside while the inside is gooey and soft. It is also very salty: soak it in water to reduce the saltiness if desired, and avoid adding any extra salt to dishes that include it.

SERVES 4

Paneer & peas in mild curry

250 g shelled peas
  (fresh or frozen)

2 tablespoons ghee or oil

150 g paneer, cut into small
  cubes

1 medium-sized onion,
  finely chopped

2 teaspoons grated fresh ginger

3 spring onions, sliced

1–2 fresh hot green chillies,
  deseeded and chopped

1 teaspoon salt

1 teaspoon garam masala

½ teaspoon sugar

chopped fresh coriander
  or mint, to serve

Boil peas in lightly salted water until almost cooked (about 3–4 minutes for fresh peas, about 1 minute for frozen peas). Drain, reserving ½ cup of the cooking water.

Heat ghee or oil in a non-stick frying pan over medium heat and fry paneer until golden. Remove with a slotted spoon and set aside. Fry onion in the same oil for about 4 minutes, until soft and lightly coloured, then increase heat to medium–high. Add ginger, spring onions, chillies, salt, garam masala and sugar, and cook for 1 minute, stirring constantly. Return peas and paneer to the pan with the reserved cooking water. Simmer gently for about 3 minutes, until flavours are absorbed.

Serve with fresh coriander or mint scattered on top.

SERVES 4

Persian eggs

1 tablespoon olive oil

1 small onion, finely chopped

1 clove garlic, crushed

½ teaspoon cumin seeds

900 g vine-ripened tomatoes, peeled and chopped

½ teaspoon ground coriander

salt and freshly ground black pepper

4 eggs

slices of multigrain bread, to serve

1 tablespoon finely chopped fresh chives, to serve

Heat oil in a large non-stick frying pan over medium–high heat. When hot, add onion, garlic and cumin seeds and sauté for a few minutes. Cover, reduce heat and cook for a further 3–4 minutes until onion is softened. Add tomatoes and ground coriander and simmer, uncovered, for about 8 minutes, until thickened. Season with salt and freshly ground pepper.

Make a small hollow in the sauce near the edge of the pan and carefully break an egg into it. Then repeat with the remaining eggs, leaving space between each. Partially cover the pan and continue to simmer for a few more minutes until eggs are cooked to your liking.

Toast bread and cut into fingers.

Serve sauce and eggs on warmed plates, scattered with chives, and with toast fingers on the side for dipping.

SERVES 2–4

Ricotta & rocket pesto pies

100 g ricotta

1 egg, lightly beaten

salt and freshly ground
   black pepper

ROCKET PESTO

2 cups chopped rocket

3 tablespoons pine nuts, toasted

2 cloves garlic, crushed

2 tablespoons extra virgin
   olive oil

salt and freshly ground
   black pepper

2 tablespoons grated
   parmesan cheese

To make the pesto, place rocket, nuts, garlic, oil and salt and freshly ground pepper in a blender or food processor and blend until it forms a thick, chunky paste. Stir in grated parmesan cheese. Cover and set aside.

Preheat oven to 180°C. Lightly grease a six-hole muffin pan.

Mix ricotta and egg until combined. Season with salt and pepper to taste. Put 2 teaspoons of rocket pesto in the bottom of each muffin cup, then spoon in ricotta mix.

Bake for 35–45 minutes or until ricotta is just firm and lightly golden on top.

Leave to cool, then unmould. Serve at room temperature with a green salad, extra pesto and crusty bread. These are great for picnics.

SERVES 6

Tomato, ricotta & mustard tarts

2 sheets ready-rolled puff pastry, defrosted

150–200 g ricotta

50 g fetta

freshly ground black pepper

3 tablespoons wholegrain mustard

4 vine-ripened tomatoes, thickly sliced

a few torn basil leaves, to serve

Preheat oven to 200°C. Lightly grease a non-stick baking tray with oil.

Use a biscuit cutter or drinking glass to cut 6-cm rounds from the pastry. For each tart, place one round on top of another and press lightly to make a double layer. Place these rounds onto the prepared baking tray.

Mash ricotta and fetta in a bowl with freshly ground pepper. Apply a thick layer of this mixture to each pastry round, then spread on a generous amount of mustard. Place a tomato slice on top of each round.

Bake tarts for 15–20 minutes, until pastry is puffed and golden.

Serve immediately, with torn basil leaves to garnish and a green salad on the side (a spinach salad with toasted walnuts is perfect).

🍄 You can substitute soft goat's cheese for the ricotta and fetta if desired.

SERVES 4–5

Zucchini, goat's cheese & baby pea frittata

500 g zucchinis, cut into 1-cm slices

2 tablespoons olive oil

1 clove garlic, crushed

8 large eggs

salt and freshly ground black pepper

1 cup shelled baby peas (preferably fresh, but frozen can be used)

½ cup torn fresh basil leaves

60 g grated parmesan cheese

125 g goat's cheese

Steam zucchini slices, or plunge into boiling water for 1–2 minutes, until just starting to cook but still crisp. Drain and pat dry.

Heat oil in a large non-stick frying pan over medium heat, add garlic and sauté for 1–2 minutes. Increase heat, add zucchini and quickly sauté for 2–3 minutes until starting to brown.

Put eggs, salt and freshly ground pepper into a bowl and whisk until just combined (it shouldn't be too frothy). Stir in peas and basil. Pour this egg mixture over the zucchini in the pan, sprinkle with parmesan cheese and scatter small spoonfuls of goat's cheese evenly over the top. Reduce heat and cook for about 6 minutes.

While the frittata is cooking, preheat the grill to high.

Place pan under the grill and cook until the egg is almost set and it is lightly browned on top. The eggs should be creamy – be careful not to overcook (it will continue to cook as it cools).

Remove from grill and set aside to cool a little before serving. Cut into wedges and serve warm or at room temperature.

🍄 If you use frozen peas, let them thaw a little before adding them.

SERVES 4

Tofu

Tofu – also known as bean curd – is made from soybeans. It is rich in protein and amino acids and is easily digested. Its bland taste makes it an excellent base to absorb other flavours, especially the unique sweet and sour tang of many south-east Asian dishes and the subtle flavours of Japanese cuisine.

Several types of tofu are available. Firm tofu is ideal for stir-frys, kebabs, salads and mashed for burgers. The much softer and quite delicate 'silken tofu' can be used in broths, or mashed to make a light sauce, almost like a cream, to use with fruit or sweet deserts. Fried 'puffed' tofu can be used in salads, stir-frys and laksas.

Try to buy organic tofu, or very fresh tofu from Asian grocery stores. Vacuum-packed and refrigerated tofu has a long shelf life. Fresh firm tofu is usually sold covered with water; change the water daily to keep it fresh.

< Baked tofu and green bean salad (page 50)

Baked tofu & green bean salad

225 g firm organic tofu, cut into
  3-cm cubes

1 teaspoon grated fresh ginger

2 cloves garlic, crushed

3 tablespoons soy sauce

3 tablespoons fresh lemon juice

350 g green beans, trimmed

2 cups mixed salad leaves

250 g cherry tomatoes, halved

2 spring onions, sliced

2 tablespoons chopped flat-leaf
  parsley

2 tablespoons sesame seeds,
  toasted

DRESSING

½ cup tahini

2 tablespoons sesame oil

2 tablespoons rice wine vinegar

2 tablespoons soy sauce

2 tablespoons fresh lemon juice

1 tablespoon warm water

Place tofu in a shallow bowl, add ginger, garlic, soy sauce and lemon juice and toss gently to coat tofu. Cover and marinate in the refrigerator for at least 1 hour, turning occasionally.

Preheat oven to 180°C. Lightly grease a baking dish with oil.

Spoon tofu onto prepared dish and bake for about 30 minutes, turning once during cooking.

Steam or boil green beans for 4–5 minutes. Rinse under cold water to stop cooking and drain well.

To make tahini dressing, combine all ingredients in a small bowl and whisk to blend.

Place salad leaves in a serving bowl, add green beans, cherry tomatoes, spring onions and half the dressing. Toss to combine.

Arrange baked tofu on top, drizzle over remaining dressing and sprinkle with parsley and sesame seeds. Serve immediately.

SERVES 4 | VEGAN

Balinese tofu
with fried rice noodles

100 g vermicelli rice noodles

4 small red shallots,
  finely chopped

2 cloves garlic, crushed

1 teaspoon salt

freshly ground black pepper

pinch of ground nutmeg

2 tablespoons vegetable oil

1 cinnamon stick

2 tomatoes, diced

400 g firm organic tofu,
  cut into large cubes

2 tablespoons kecap manis

1 cup water

2 spring onions, finely sliced
  on an angle

4 lime wedges

Place the noodles in a small saucepan or bowl, cover with boiling water
and leave to soak for 5 minutes. Drain well.

Place shallots, garlic, salt, pepper and nutmeg in a mortar and grind to
a paste. Heat oil in a wok over medium–high heat until just smoking. Add
garlic paste and cinnamon stick and stir-fry for 2 minutes or until fragrant.
Add tomatoes and tofu and stir-fry for 1 minute. Add kecap manis and
water and bring to the boil. Take off the heat and remove cinnamon stick.
Add noodles and toss gently until heated through.

Divide noodles among serving bowls, sprinkle with spring onions and serve
with a wedge of lime.

SERVES 4 | VEGAN

Pad Thai

250 g rice stick noodles

¼ cup tamarind paste

¼ cup warm water

3 tablespoons soy sauce

2 tablespoons sugar

2 tablespoons fresh lime juice

6 tablespoons roasted peanuts

¼ cup vegetable oil

2 cloves garlic, chopped

½ red chilli, deseeded and
  sliced

100 g firm organic tofu, cut into
  1-cm cubes

2 eggs, lightly beaten

1 cup bean sprouts

2 spring onions, cut into
  2-cm pieces

½ red capsicum, deseeded and
  thinly sliced

fresh coriander leaves, to serve

lime wedges, to serve

Soak noodles in plenty of cold water for 40–60 minutes.

Put tamarind paste in a small bowl with ¼ cup warm water and soak for 15–20 minutes. Then mash and push through a sieve (discard any solids in the sieve). Mix the strained tamarind juice with the soy sauce, sugar and lime juice.

Put peanuts into a blender or grinder and process until ground. Set aside.

Heat oil in a large non-stick frying pan or wok over high heat until it is almost smoking. (As you add the remaining ingredients, make sure to keep the heat high and work quickly so the noodles don't become sticky and overcooked.) Add garlic and stir for about 30 seconds. Add chilli and tofu and stir-fry for 1 minute. Tip eggs into wok and fry for 1–2 minutes.

Drain noodles and add to wok, stir-frying and working in the egg mix (the egg will coat the noodles). Add tamarind and lime juice mixture and continue stir-frying for a further 1–2 minutes.

Add about two-thirds of the ground peanuts, about two-thirds of the bean sprouts and the spring onions. Stir-fry for 30 seconds and remove from heat.

Transfer noodles to a warmed serving dish and sprinkle with remaining ground peanuts and bean sprouts, strips of red capsicum and fresh coriander leaves.

Serve immediately with lime wedges on the side.

SERVES 2–3

Rice paper rolls with dipping sauce

1 tablespoon sunflower or
    peanut oil

200 g firm organic tofu, cut into
    strips

100 g vermicelli rice noodles

1 packet large dried rice-paper
    wrappers

2 cups shredded iceberg lettuce

1 carrot, peeled and cut into
    long matchsticks

½ cup fresh Thai basil leaves

1 cup fresh coriander leaves

4 spring onions, trimmed and
    cut into strips lengthways

DIPPING SAUCE

¼ cup rice wine vinegar

¼ cup water

1 teaspoon soy sauce

1 teaspoon caster sugar

1 teaspoon sesame seeds, toasted

1 small red chilli, deseeded and
    finely sliced

To make dipping sauce, combine all ingredients in a small bowl and mix well.

Then heat oil in a non-stick frying pan or wok over medium–high heat. Add
tofu strips and cook for 3–4 minutes until lightly browned. Set aside.

Cover vermicelli noodles with boiling water and leave to soak for 5 minutes.
Strain, then gently separate noodles.

Pour some very hot water into a large shallow bowl. Place a rice-paper
wrapper in the water, leave for about 30 seconds until soft, then carefully
lift out and place on a clean dry tea towel or chopping board.   >

In the centre of the wrapper, lay some noodles, lettuce, tofu strips, carrot sticks, herbs and spring onion. Fold two sides of the rice paper wrapper over the filling to form the ends, then take the side closest to you and roll it tightly over the filling to make a neat parcel. Press down edge (add a little extra water if necessary) to seal. Repeat with remaining ingredients.

When rolls are made, cover with a damp tea-towel or cling wrap to keep fresh and moist until serving.

Serve with dipping sauce.

SERVES 4 | VEGAN

Soy burgers

1 × 400-g can soybeans, drained and rinsed

450 g organic tofu, chopped

1 clove garlic, chopped

2 spring onions, sliced

½ cup chopped flat-leaf parsley

1 teaspoon Dijon mustard

2 cups fresh breadcrumbs

salt

vegetable oil, for frying

Place soybeans, tofu, garlic, spring onions, parsley and mustard in a blender or food processor and blend until combined but still chunky. Transfer to a bowl, add breadcrumbs and mix. Season with salt. Shape mixture into about eight round, flat patties.

Heat oil in a large non-stick frying pan over medium–high heat. Add two or three patties at a time and cook for about 10 minutes, turning once, until golden brown.

Serve with avocado and lime salsa (page 222) and a green salad, or in a toasted roll with lettuce and sweet tomato chutney (page 238).

🍄 To make fresh breadcrumbs, whiz day-old bread in the blender for a few minutes. Multigrain bread adds some extra nuttiness to the burgers.

SERVES 4 | VEGAN

Spiced tofu & Asian herb salad

2 tablespoons sesame seeds

½ teaspoon chilli flakes

1 teaspoon ground star anise

600 g organic tofu, thickly sliced

1 tablespoon peanut or
    sunflower oil

2 Lebanese cucumbers,
    thinly sliced

2 cups bean sprouts

1 cup fresh Thai basil leaves

1 cup fresh coriander leaves

DRESSING

3 tablespoons rice wine vinegar

½ cup fresh lime juice

2 tablespoons caster sugar

To make the sweet and sour dressing, place all ingredients in a small bowl and whisk with a fork until sugar is dissolved.

Then combine sesame seeds, chilli flakes and star anise. Pat tofu dry, then sprinkle with spice mix.

Heat oil in a non-stick frying pan over medium heat and fry tofu for about 4 minutes on each side, turning carefully, until cooked.

Place tofu in a large salad bowl and add sliced cucumbers, bean sprouts and fresh herbs. Mix gently and then divide between four plates. Pour dressing over salad.

SERVES 4

Tofu & red capsicum satay

900 g extra-firm organic tofu

1 red capsicum, deseeded and
cut into 6-cm squares

3 tablespoons soy sauce

2 tablespoons light sesame oil

1 tablespoon grated fresh ginger

bamboo skewers, soaked in
water for 30 minutes before
using

PEANUT SAUCE

1 tablespoon peanut oil

2 cloves garlic, crushed

½ cup crunchy peanut butter

¼ teaspoon chilli flakes

1½ tablespoons palm sugar
or soft brown sugar

¾ cup coconut milk

To make peanut sauce, heat oil in a small saucepan over medium heat.
Add garlic and sauté for 1 minute until beginning to soften. Add peanut
butter, chilli, sugar and coconut milk and stir until combined and heated
through. Set aside.

Pat tofu dry with paper towel, then cut into 6-cm cubes. Place in a shallow
bowl with the capsicum.

Mix soy sauce, sesame oil and grated ginger in a small bowl, then pour this
marinade over the tofu and red capsicum and toss lightly to coat. Cover,
then leave to marinate in the refrigerator for several hours or overnight.

Preheat barbecue or oven grill to high. ➤

Thread tofu and red capsicum onto soaked skewers. Barbecue or grill for 10–15 minutes, turning occasionally, until golden brown. Brush with a little of the marinade while cooking.

Serve warm or at room temperature with warm peanut sauce, steamed rice and a leafy salad.

🍄 Make sure to soak the skewers before using, otherwise they will burn.

SERVES 6 | VEGAN

Tofu & vegetable curry

2 tablespoons vegetable oil

500 g firm organic tofu, cut into
  3-cm cubes

1 × 400-ml can coconut milk

¼ cup soy sauce

1 teaspoon grated fresh ginger

½ teaspoon soft brown sugar

1½ teaspoons curry powder

2 teaspoons chilli paste

1 green capsicum, deseeded
  and thinly sliced

4 spring onions, sliced

120 g baby sweet corn, cut into
  2 cm lengths

2–3 baby bok choy, trimmed
  and chopped

½ cup chopped fresh coriander

salt to taste

steamed rice, to serve

Heat oil in a large non-stick frying pan or wok and fry tofu over medium–
high heat for about 3 minutes on each side, until lightly browned. Set aside
and keep warm.

Combine coconut milk, soy sauce, ginger, sugar, curry powder and chilli
paste in the frying pan or wok and bring slowly to the boil. Add green
capsicum, spring onions, baby corn and tofu, cover and simmer for about
5 minutes. Add bok choy and coriander and cook for a further 3–4 minutes,
until bok choy is just wilted. Check for seasoning and add a little salt if
needed.

To serve, pile steamed rice in bowls and spoon curry over the top.

SERVES 6 | VEGAN

Pasta & noodles

Pasta and noodles are wholesome, filling and easy to cook —
and it's amazing how many variations there can be! For those
who think they might be left hungry if they don't eat meat,
pasta is the answer. You can add the simplest sauce of oven-
roasted tomatoes, or pile it high with vegetables and beans,
cheese and herbs. Pasta can't hide its Italian origins and its
sense of good, healthy home cooking.

Most pasta is wheat-based, and the best pasta is made from
hard-grained durum wheat that does not become mushy
when you cook it. However, it's also possible to buy rice-
based, corn-based and even vegetable pastas.

Noodles provide similar options — from wheat and rice noodles to buckwheat noodles. They're an excellent foil for
myriad flavours. And noodles positively shine in a soothing
broth or spicy stir-fry.

< Farfalle with garlic, potatoes & spinach (page 68)

Farfalle with garlic, potatoes & spinach

¼ cup virgin olive oil

3 cloves garlic, chopped

1 small red chilli, deseeded and sliced

500 g small waxy potatoes, cut into 1-cm slices

400 g farfalle (butterfly-shaped pasta)

200 g baby spinach leaves, stalks removed

2 tablespoons grated parmesan cheese, to serve

Heat oil in a small, non-stick frying pan over low heat. Add garlic and chilli and sauté for 4–5 minutes until garlic is softened.

Cook potato slices in boiling water for about 10 minutes or until tender. Drain and set aside.

Cook farfalle in plenty of salted boiling water according to packet instructions until al dente. Drain, reserving 2–3 tablespoons of the cooking liquid. Tip pasta back into the saucepan with reserved liquid, add potatoes, garlic mix and spinach and stir until spinach is softened.

Serve immediately in warmed bowls, with a sprinkling of parmesan on top.

SERVES 4 | VEGAN: OMIT PARMESAN CHEESE

Lasagne with spinach & mushrooms

1 tablespoon olive oil

1 clove garlic, chopped

1 small brown onion, chopped

1 × 800-g can chopped tomatoes

½ cup vegetable stock

1 tablespoon chopped fresh oregano

250 g ricotta

1 tablespoon chopped fresh basil

½ teaspoon freshly grated nutmeg

salt and freshly ground black pepper

1 × 250-g packet dried lasagne sheets

250 g cooked drained chopped spinach (about 1 large bunch fresh spinach, or use frozen spinach)

300 g button mushrooms, thinly sliced

200 g mozzarella cheese, grated

Heat oil in a non-stick saucepan over medium–high heat. Add garlic and onion and sauté for 1–2 minutes. Add chopped tomatoes, stock and oregano. Bring to the boil, then reduce heat and simmer for about 10 minutes. Leave to cool a little.

Preheat oven to 180°C.

Put ricotta in a bowl, add chopped basil and grated nutmeg, season with salt and freshly ground pepper and mix well. >

Spoon a thin layer of tomato sauce over the base of a 22-cm × 28-cm ovenproof dish. Place a single layer of pasta sheets on top, spread over half the ricotta mix, then arrange the spinach in an even layer, add another layer of pasta sheets and spoon over some tomato sauce. Spread remaining ricotta mix on top, then arrange mushrooms in a layer on top, followed by a layer of pasta sheets. Cover the lasagne with remaining tomato sauce (make sure pasta sheets are completely moistened by the sauce).

Cover the dish with aluminium foil and bake for 30 minutes. Remove from the oven and sprinkle grated mozzarella over the top. Return to the oven, uncovered, for 15–20 minutes, until cheese is bubbling and lightly browned in spots. Use a skewer to make sure pasta is cooked through.

Remove from oven, cover with foil and set aside for 5–10 minutes before serving.

🍄 If your baking dish is a different size to that specified, just snap the pasta sheets to size so they fit neatly in a single layer.

SERVES 4–6

Linguine with roast pumpkin & fetta

500 g pumpkin, peeled and
   cut into 2-cm cubes

salt and freshly ground
   black pepper

3 tablespoons olive oil

2 tablespoons fresh lemon juice

1 teaspoon finely grated
   lemon zest

125 g fetta

1 cup small fresh basil leaves

400 g linguine

2 cups baby spinach leaves,
   stalks removed

Preheat oven to 200°C.

Put pumpkin in a bowl, season with salt and freshly ground pepper and
add 1 tablespoon of the oil. Toss to coat. Tip onto a non-stick baking tray,
spread out and roast for 15 minutes.

Meanwhile, put remaining olive oil, lemon juice and zest, fetta and basil
in a bowl and toss to combine.

Cook linguine in plenty of salted boiling water according to packet
instructions until al dente. Drain and return to pan. Add spinach, fetta
mixture and roasted pumpkin and toss until spinach wilts.

Serve immediately in warmed bowls.

SERVES 4

Mushroom noodle salad

2 teaspoons sesame oil

¼ cup rice wine vinegar

¼ cup tamari

2 tablespoons fresh lemon juice

1 tablespoon finely grated lemon zest

1 teaspoon grated fresh ginger

3 spring onions, sliced

1 clove garlic, crushed

3 tablespoons chopped fresh coriander

¼ teaspoon chilli flakes (optional)

300 g button mushrooms, sliced

300 g dried ramen noodles

¼ cup roasted peanuts, chopped

extra chopped fresh coriander, to serve

Put sesame oil, rice wine vinegar, tamari, lemon juice, lemon zest, ginger, spring onions, garlic, coriander and chilli flakes in a large bowl and stir to combine. Add sliced mushrooms and toss to coat. Set aside for 15 minutes to marinate.

Cook noodles according to packet directions, then rinse in cold water to stop cooking and drain. Add noodles to the mushroom mixture and toss to combine. Cover and refrigerate for at least 1 hour for flavours to develop.

Before serving, toss again (the noodles will soak up the dressing, so if they seem too dry add a little extra lemon juice and soy sauce). Serve at room temperature, with peanuts and extra coriander scattered over the top.

SERVES 4

Pasta with mushrooms & mascarpone

50 g butter

2 cloves garlic, crushed

500 g medium-sized field mushrooms, sliced

250 g mascarpone

salt and freshly ground pepper

400 g dried pasta (such as linguine)

2 tablespoons chopped flat-leaf parsley

Heat butter in a large non-stick frying pan over medium heat. Add garlic and sauté for 1 minute. Add mushrooms and stir until they start to release their juices and brown. Reduce heat, stir in mascarpone and continue to stir until it forms a sauce. If sauce is a little thick, add 1–2 tablespoons of water. Check sauce for seasoning and add salt and freshly ground pepper if needed.

Meanwhile, cook pasta in plenty of salted boiling water according to packet instructions until al dente. Drain.

Add sauce to pasta, stir through parsley and serve immediately. Serve with a bitter radicchio or rocket salad with a sharp dressing, to balance the richness of the mascarpone.

SERVES 4

Pasta with walnut sauce

1 slice wholemeal bread

2 tablespoons milk

250 g walnut pieces

2 cloves garlic, crushed

pinch of ground nutmeg

salt and freshly ground
   black pepper

400 g wholemeal fettuccine

3 tablespoons butter

3 tablespoons chopped flat-leaf
   parsley, plus extra to serve

Soak the bread in the milk.

Heat a non-stick frying pan over medium heat, add walnuts and cook, stirring, for 5–6 minutes until they are lightly toasted. Leave to cool for a few minutes.

Put walnuts and garlic in a food processor or blender and pulse several times until lightly crushed. Tip nuts into a bowl, add soaked bread, nutmeg and salt and freshly ground black pepper, cover and leave for 30 minutes.

Cook fettuccine in plenty of salted boiling water according to packet instructions until al dente. Drain, but leave a little water clinging to the pasta, then tip into a warmed serving bowl, add butter and parsley, stir through walnut sauce and serve immediately with extra parsley on top.

SERVES 4 | VEGAN: USE SOY MILK AND SUBSTITUTE OIL FOR THE BUTTER

Risoni pilaf

3 cups vegetable stock

1 cup risoni

1 tablespoon butter

1 tablespoon finely chopped flat-leaf parsley

1 tablespoon chopped fresh basil leaves

salt and freshly ground black pepper

Bring stock to the boil in a medium-sized saucepan. Add risoni, stir, bring back to the boil, then reduce heat to medium and simmer for 15 minutes, stirring occasionally. Reduce heat to low and cook for a few more minutes until stock is absorbed.

Take off heat, stir in butter, fresh herbs, salt and freshly ground pepper. Cover and leave for 2–3 minutes before serving.

SERVES 4 | VEGAN: SUBSTITUTE OIL FOR THE BUTTER

Risoni with spinach, herbs & pine nuts

1¾ cups risoni

2 tablespoons olive oil

1 small red onion, finely chopped

1 clove garlic, crushed

300 g baby spinach leaves, stalks
   removed

½ cup finely chopped flat-leaf
   parsley

½ cup chopped fresh basil leaves

¼ cup fresh lemon juice

½ cup grated parmesan cheese

salt and freshly ground
   black pepper

½ cup pine nuts, toasted

Cook risoni in a large saucepan of salted boiling water according to packet instructions until al dente.

Meanwhile, heat oil in a large frying pan or saucepan over medium heat. Add onion and garlic and cook for 3–4 minutes until softened. Add spinach leaves, parsley and basil and stir for a few minutes until just wilted. Drain risoni and as soon as spinach is softened, stir spinach mixture through hot risoni, then stir through lemon juice and parmesan cheese.

Season with salt and freshly ground pepper, sprinkle with toasted pine nuts and serve immediately.

SERVES 4–6 | VEGAN: OMIT PARMESAN CHEESE

Soba noodle & snow pea salad

200 g snow peas, topped
and tailed

200 g soba noodles

2 spring onions, finely sliced

2 tablespoons sesame seeds,
toasted

DRESSING

½ clove garlic, crushed

1 teaspoon grated fresh ginger

1 tablespoon olive oil

1 teaspoon sesame oil

1 tablespoon tahini

1 teaspoon tamari

1½ tablespoons rice wine
vinegar

1 tablespoon warm water

2 teaspoons caster sugar

Place snow peas in a small saucepan of boiling water and cook for 1 minute. Drain and rinse under cold water or place into iced water to stop cooking (they should still be quite crisp). Drain. Slice the snow peas on an angle into thin strips.

Place noodles in a medium-sized saucepan of boiling water and cook for 3–4 minutes, or until tender. Drain, rinse under cold water and drain again.

To make the tahini dressing, place all ingredients in a small screw-top jar, and shake until well combined. Place noodles and snow peas in a bowl, pour over dressing and toss to combine. Scatter over spring onions and sesame seeds and serve.

SERVES 4–6 | VEGAN

Spaghettini with avocado, lime & almonds

¼ cup slivered almonds

1 large avocado, peeled and stoned

¼ cup fresh lime juice

400 g spaghettini

3 tablespoons olive oil

½ cup fresh coriander leaves, to serve

Place almonds in a frying pan over high heat and dry-fry until lightly toasted.

Dice avocado, place in a small bowl and pour over a little of the lime juice to stop it from browning.

Cook spaghettini in plenty of salted boiling water until al dente. Heat oil in a small frying pan. Drain pasta and tip back into saucepan, add hot oil, almonds and avocado, stir quickly and divide between four warm serving bowls. Pour over remaining lime juice and sprinkle with coriander leaves. Serve immediately.

Spaghettini is thinner than spaghetti and is perfect with this delicate sauce. If you can't find it, use another fine pasta.

SERVES 4 | VEGAN

Spaghetti with spring vegetables

350 g shelled fresh broad beans

300 g fresh asparagus spears, trimmed (see note on page 178)

200 g sugar snap peas, topped and tailed

400 g wholemeal spaghetti

2 tablespoons unsalted butter

1 clove garlic, crushed

2 tablespoons fresh lemon juice

salt and freshly ground black pepper

2 tablespoons shaved parmesan cheese

Bring a large saucepan of water to the boil, add broad beans and cook for 2–3 minutes. Drain, rinse under cold water then use your fingers to pop off the skins.

Cut asparagus spears on an angle into 3-cm lengths. Bring some fresh water to the boil, add asparagus pieces and cook for 2 minutes. Add sugar snap peas and cook for another minute. Drain.

Cook spaghetti in plenty of salted boiling water according to packet instructions until al dente.

While spaghetti is cooking, heat butter in a large frying pan, add garlic and stir for 1–2 minutes. Add cooked vegetables, lemon juice, salt and freshly ground pepper and toss to combine. Immediately add drained spaghetti and toss gently. Serve immediately with shaved parmesan.

 Sugar snap peas are small, crunchy and delicious and, like snow peas, are eaten without shelling.

SERVES 6

Vegetable laksa

CURRY PASTE

2 cloves garlic, crushed

2-cm piece galangal, peeled
  and chopped

2 stalks lemongrass, outer leaves
  stripped and centre
  finely chopped

1 green chilli, finely sliced

1 tablespoon soy sauce

2 tablespoons raw peanuts

1 teaspoon ground turmeric

1 teaspoon ground coriander

SOUP

250 g thick Hokkien noodles

2 tablespoons vegetable oil

1 litre vegetable stock

1 × 400-ml can coconut milk

300 g puffed tofu, cut into
  3-cm cubes

1 teaspoon grated lime zest

50 g snow peas, finely sliced
  on an angle

2 spring onions, finely sliced
  on an angle

1 cup bean shoots

salt

2 tablespoons fresh
  coriander leaves

lime wedges, to serve

Grind all paste ingredients in a blender or mortar to make a thick paste.

Cook noodles according to packet instructions, drain and set aside. >

Heat oil in a frying pan, add curry paste and fry for a few minutes until fragrant. Add stock and coconut milk and bring almost to the boil, then reduce heat and simmer for 5 minutes. Add puffed tofu, lime zest, snow peas and spring onions and simmer for a further 2 minutes. Add bean shoots and cook for 1 minute. Check for seasoning and add a little salt if needed.

Divide cooked noodles between four bowls, then ladle in soup. Scatter coriander leaves on top and serve with lime wedges on the side.

🍄 A traditional laksa would have shrimp paste (or blachan), a salty and quite fishy paste which, used sparingly, provides an intangible and authentic aroma and flavour. If you are not a strict vegetarian you might like to use 1 teaspoon of this in the curry paste instead of the soy sauce.

SERVES 4 | VEGAN

Vermicelli with balsamic-roasted tomatoes

400 g vine-ripened cherry truss tomatoes
  (or use small tomatoes)
1 clove garlic, halved
3 tablespoons balsamic vinegar
1 tablespoon soft brown sugar
freshly ground black pepper
400 g vermicelli
2 tablespoons chopped flat leaf parsley, to serve

Preheat oven to 160°C.

Place tomatoes and garlic in a small roasting dish. Pour balsamic vinegar over, sprinkle with sugar, season with pepper and toss to combine. Roast for 20–25 minutes, basting occasionally.

Meanwhile, cook vermicelli in plenty of salted boiling water according to packet instructions. Drain.

Divide pasta into warmed bowls, top with roasted tomatoes and spoon over juices. Scatter with chopped parsley.

SERVES 4 | VEGAN

Grains & pulses

If vegetables are the heart of vegetarian cooking, pulses and grains are the body and soul. Nutritious and fibre-rich, they're low in fat, hearty and filling. They provide almost infinite possibilities for every meal of the day and have had a starring role in cuisines around the world for centuries.

Pulses such as dried beans, peas and lentils are great pantry stand-bys and offer diverse flavours and textures. Store pulses and grains in airtight containers in a cool place, and remember that these are natural products without preservatives, so they don't last forever. Note that all the recipes here use dried pulses, unless otherwise specified.

Rice is a staple food for more than half the world's population, and it comes in many shapes and forms. But there are many other grains to try — wheat (including cracked wheat and couscous), polenta (made from corn), buckwheat and quinoa to mention a few.

< Basic couscous (page 95)

How to cook pulses

- Pick over dried beans, peas and lentils before cooking to remove any small stones or discoloured or shrivelled beans.
- Rinse well under running water before use.
- Soaking speeds up the cooking time. Some beans, such as chickpeas, need to be soaked for 6–8 hours or overnight. Lentils and split peas usually don't need any soaking before cooking.
- To soak pulses: cover with enough water to reach 4 cm above pulses and leave to soak for 6–12 hours (overnight is usually best).
- After soaking, drain pulses, place in a saucepan and cover with fresh water (again, there should be around 3–4 cm of water above the beans). Bring to the boil, skim any scum from the surface, reduce heat and simmer until beans are tender. (See the list opposite: most beans take about an hour to cook but timing depends on the variety and also on the freshness of the beans.)

- Only add salt after the pulses are cooked or near the end of the cooking time.
- Add bay leaves, herbs, onion or spices to the water when cooking, for extra flavour.
- You can reduce the soaking time by boiling the legumes for about 10 minutes before soaking. However, this will sometimes cause the skins to split when they are cooking.

SOME AVERAGE COOKING TIMES FOR DRIED BEANS (AFTER SOAKING):

Black beans	1 hour
Black-eyed beans	1–1¼ hours
Borlotti	1–1½ hours
Broad beans	1½ hours
Butter/lima beans	1–1¼ hours
Cannellini beans	1 hour
Chickpeas	1½–2 hours
Kidney beans	1–1½ hours
Mung beans	1–1¼ hours
Soybeans	2 hours

Canned beans

If you are short of time, canned beans and other pulses can be a quick way to create an easy healthy meal, but they can be very salty and a bit mushy. Chickpeas and kidney beans are two of the best canned pulses as they seem to stay quite firm. Canned beans are particularly good for dips, burgers or patties (when they are to be mashed anyway) or when added to a soup at the last moment.

Read the label and check that the canned beans do not contain sugar or other unnecessary additives. Always drain and rinse them well before use.

Basic couscous

2 cups couscous
salt
2 cups boiling water
1 tablespoon butter

Place couscous and salt in a small bowl. Pour over boiling water and cover bowl with cling wrap. Leave in a warm place for 5 minutes to allow grains to expand. Add butter and fluff with a fork to separate grains.

🌿 Couscous is made from semolina and wheat, which have been rubbed together to form small grains. There are a number of varieties but the most common is a fine-grain couscous. You can use couscous as you would rice. Use vegetable stock instead of water to add more flavour, or stir through toasted nuts, currants and chopped herbs for a change.

SERVES 4–6 | VEGAN

Basic quinoa

1 cup quinoa

1½ cups water

½ teaspoon salt

butter (optional)

Rinse the quinoa several times, using fresh water each time, then drain. Place in a small saucepan with 1½ cups fresh water and salt. Bring to the boil, reduce heat, cover and simmer for 20 minutes.

Remove from heat and leave, covered, for about 5 minutes. Use a fork to separate the grains and add a little butter if you like.

🍄 Quinoa (pronounced keen-wah) is a light grain that is high in protein and fibre. As it has no wheat it is suitable of those on a gluten-free or low-gluten diet. Quinoa is quite high in oil and should be stored in a sealed container in the refrigerator. Serve as you would rice or couscous. Add toasted nuts or seeds and serve like a pilaf, or add chopped parsley and tomato and make a quinoa 'tabbouleh' (for the recipe on page 174, just substitute quinoa for the cracked wheat).

SERVES 4 | VEGAN

Basic rice

1 cup white or brown rice
1½–3 cups water

To use the absorption method: rinse and drain rice to remove some starch, if desired. Place rice and 1½–2 cups water in a saucepan, stir, then bring to the boil. Once boiling, lower heat to medium, cover and simmer (simmer white rice for 15–20 minutes; simmer brown rice for 25–30 minutes). Remove from heat, leave covered and stand for at least 5–10 minutes. Fluff with a fork and serve. (The absorption method is recommended for making the fluffiest rice. If cooking a large quantity of rice using this method, the amount of water may need to be reduced.)

To use the rapid-boil method: rinse and drain rice to remove some starch, if desired. Place rice and 3 cups water in a saucepan, stir, then bring to the boil. Reduce heat and simmer gently, uncovered (simmer white rice for 10 minutes; simmer brown rice for 20–25 minutes). Drain, cover with a lid and leave to stand for at least 5–10 minutes. Fluff with a fork and serve. >

There are literally thousands of varieties of rice, from fragrant jasmine and aromatic basmati to delicate long-grain red rice and even the ebony-coloured black rice, which is often served in Asia as a sweet dish. Wild rice is actually a grass, but is cooked and served like rice, often mixed with other rice varieties. The three main categories of rice are short, medium and long grain, and the different shapes and qualities of the grain suit different dishes (e.g. short and starchy for risotto; long and fine to accompany curries). Risotto rice should not be cooked using the absorption or rapid-boil methods, and should not be rinsed before use (see pages 136–8 for how to cook risotto).

MAKES 3 CUPS WHITE RICE OR 3½ CUPS BROWN RICE

Basmati with peas

2 tablespoons vegetable oil

4 cloves

4 cardamom pods, crushed

4 whole black peppercorns

1 cinnamon stick

1 clove garlic, crushed

2 cups basmati rice, rinsed
and drained

1 litre water

1 cup shelled peas
(fresh or frozen)

salt

Heat oil in a heavy-based saucepan over low heat. Add cloves, cardamom pods, peppercorns and cinnamon stick. Cook, stirring, for 2–3 minutes to bring out the aroma of the spices. Add garlic and cook for 1 minute.

Add rice and water. Bring to the boil, cover and cook for about 10 minutes. Add peas, stir, then cover again and cook for a further 5 minutes until rice is tender and water has been absorbed. Take off heat and leave, covered, for 2–3 minutes.

Check for seasoning and add salt if needed. Fluff with a fork and serve.

🍄 This is an easy rice dish with a subtle Indian flavour. It's good with curry, or to add a lift to steamed vegetables. For a richer flavour, substitute butter or ghee for the oil. It's also nice with some chopped toasted pistachios or pine nuts sprinkled over before serving.

SERVES 6 | VEGAN

Black-eyed beans with chilli & herbs

225 g black-eyed beans

2 tablespoons olive oil

2 cloves garlic, finely chopped

1 small red chilli, deseeded and
   sliced

2 bay leaves

1 sprig fresh thyme

1 sprig fresh oregano

pinch of sweet paprika

salt

chopped flat-leaf parsley,
   to serve

Place beans in a bowl, cover with plenty of water and soak for at least
3 hours, or preferably overnight. Drain and place in a saucepan with plenty
of fresh water. Bring to the boil, skim surface to remove any scum, reduce
heat, partially cover and simmer for about 40 minutes or until beans are
just tender. (Do not drain.)

Heat oil in a non-stick frying pan or saucepan over medium–high heat.
Add garlic and chilli and sauté for about 1 minute. Add beans with their
cooking liquid, bay leaves, fresh herbs, paprika and salt. Stir and bring to
the boil, then reduce heat and simmer, uncovered, for about 20 minutes.

Serve sprinkled with flat-leaf parsley, with some steamed jasmine rice,
a salad and fresh bread.

SERVES 4–6 | VEGAN

Broad bean polpette

900 g shelled broad beans (fresh or frozen)
4 tablespoons chickpea flour
20 fresh mint leaves
salt and freshly ground black pepper
vegetable oil, for frying
4 lemon wedges, to serve

SAUCE
1 tablespoon Dijon mustard
1 cup natural yoghurt

If using fresh broad beans, cook in boiling water for 4–5 minutes until tender. Drain, then remove outer pod by popping it off between your finger and thumb. If beans are frozen, place them in a bowl, pour boiling water over and leave for 1 minute. Drain, then remove outer pod.

Place cooked beans in a food processor or blender with 2 tablespoons of the chickpea flour, mint leaves, salt and freshly ground pepper. Blend until mixture forms a thick paste. Shape into about eight patties, then lightly coat with remaining chickpea flour.

To make Dijon sauce, stir mustard into yoghurt to combine.

Heat a thin layer of vegetable oil in a non-stick frying pan over medium heat and shallow-fry patties for about 4 minutes on each side, or until golden brown.

Serve polpette with Dijon sauce and lemon wedges on the side.

🍄 Chickpea flour, or besan, is made from ground chickpeas and has a slightly nutty flavour. It is widely used in Indian and Middle Eastern cooking, especially for flatbreads and pancakes. It is gluten-free.

SERVES 4 | VEGAN: SUBSTITUTE SOY YOGHURT FOR NATURAL YOGHURT

Buckwheat pancakes

1 cup buttermilk

1 egg

3 tablespoons butter, melted

6 tablespoons plain flour

6 tablespoons buckwheat flour

1 teaspoon caster sugar

½ teaspoon salt

½ teaspoon bicarbonate of soda

butter or vegetable oil, for frying

In a medium bowl, whisk together buttermilk, egg and melted butter.

Sift flours into a bowl, then add sugar, salt and bicarbonate of soda. Pour buttermilk mix into dry ingredients and stir until just combined. Cover and leave for at least 30 minutes. If mixture looks too thick when you are ready to start cooking, add a little extra buttermilk.

Heat 1 tablespoon of butter or oil in a large non-stick frying pan over medium heat. When butter is melted (or oil is hot) spoon in batter to make two or three pancakes at a time, each about 8 cm across. When bubbles form on top of the pancakes, turn them over and cook for about 3 minutes on the other side, or until golden. >

You may need to add a little more butter or oil to the pan when cooking subsequent batches. Don't let the pan become too hot or the pancakes will burn.

Serve warm, with sweet or savoury toppings.

Buckwheat pancakes are great with grilled tomatoes and scrambled eggs. Try them with poached pears and yoghurt drizzled with honey, or with homemade jam.

SERVES 2–3

Chickpea & fetta patties

1 × 400-g can chickpeas,
  rinsed and drained (or 150 g
  dried chickpeas, cooked,
  see pages 92–93)

½ teaspoon ground coriander

½ teaspoon ground cumin

1 egg

2 tablespoons plain flour

2 spring onions, thinly sliced

2 tablespoons chopped fresh
  coriander

200 g fetta, crumbled

salt and freshly ground
  black pepper

olive oil, for frying

SALAD

2 cups mixed salad leaves

¼ cup chopped fresh mint
  leaves

¼ cup vinaigrette (page 242)

SAUCE

¾ cup natural yoghurt

2 tablespoons fresh lemon juice

1 teaspoon grated lemon zest

To make lemon yoghurt sauce, combine yoghurt, lemon juice and zest
in a small bowl, cover and refrigerate until needed.

To make patties, place chickpeas, spices, egg, flour and spring onions
in a blender or food processor and blend until almost smooth. Spoon the
chickpea mixture into a bowl, add coriander and fetta and stir to combine.
Check seasoning and add salt and freshly ground pepper if needed
(if using canned chickpeas it may be quite salty already). **>**

Form the mixture into small patties. Heat olive oil in a non-stick frying pan over medium heat and shallow-fry patties for 2–3 minutes on each side, until brown. Drain on paper towel.

Place salad leaves and mint leaves in a bowl. Pour over vinaigrette and toss to combine. Arrange salad on four plates. Top with fritters and drizzle over some lemon yoghurt sauce. Serve immediately.

SERVES 4

Cinnamon couscous
with pistachios & barberries

2¼ cups couscous

2¼ cups vegetable stock

1 cinnamon stick

2 tablespoons olive oil

1 onion, finely chopped

1 teaspoon ground cinnamon

1 teaspoon ground cumin

4 tablespoons dried barberries

2 tablespoons water

1½ tablespoons unsalted butter, melted

3 tablespoons finely chopped flat-leaf parsley

3 tablespoons chopped roasted unsalted pistachios

Place couscous in a large bowl. Heat stock with cinnamon stick in a saucepan until boiling. Pour boiling stock over couscous (it should completely cover the couscous – add a little extra boiling water if necessary) then cover and leave for 10 minutes.

Meanwhile, heat oil in a frying pan over medium heat and sauté onion for a few minutes until softened. Add ground cinnamon, cumin, barberries and 2 tablespoons water and cook, stirring, until liquid is almost absorbed.

Use a fork to fluff up couscous, then stir through butter, parsley, and barberry mixture. Pile onto a serving platter and scatter over pistachios. >

Barberries are a small dried fruit often used in Middle Eastern cooking. They are available from Middle Eastern food stores and specialist delis. If you can't find them, use dried cranberries. This couscous goes well with roast vegetables.

SERVES 4–6 | VEGAN: SUBSTITUTE OLIVE OIL FOR BUTTER

Couscous & chilli patties

1 cup couscous

1 cup boiling water

2 tablespoons olive oil

3 spring onions, finely sliced

1 red chilli, deseeded and finely
  sliced

3 tablespoons chopped fresh
  coriander

3 tablespoons Greek yoghurt

1 egg, lightly beaten

salt and freshly ground
  black pepper

lemon wedges, to serve

Put couscous in a small bowl, pour over boiling water, cover and leave
for 10 minutes.

Meanwhile, heat 1 tablespoon olive oil in a large non-stick frying pan over
medium heat. Add spring onions and chilli and cook for about 1 minute.

Use a fork to fluff up couscous grains then stir through cooked onion mix,
coriander, yoghurt and egg. Season with salt and pepper. Shape spoonfuls
into small patties (they are quite fragile so try not to handle them too much).

Heat remaining oil in a non-stick frying pan and fry patties, turning once,
until golden brown.

Serve with lemon wedges.

SERVES 3–4

Couscous with broccoli & harissa

1 cup chickpeas

500 g broccoli, cut into florets

2 cups couscous

2 cups boiling water

2 tablespoons butter

3 tablespoons olive oil

2 red onions, finely chopped

2 cloves garlic, finely sliced

1 red chilli, deseeded and chopped

2 teaspoons coriander seeds

1 teaspoon ras el hanout

2 tablespoons chopped fresh coriander

2 tablespoons chopped fresh mint

2 tablespoons pine nuts, toasted

extra fresh coriander leaves, to serve

natural yoghurt, to serve

DRESSING

1 teaspoon harissa (page 228)

2–3 tablespoons vegetable stock

1 tablespoon fresh lemon juice

1 tablespoon olive oil

Place chickpeas in a bowl, cover with plenty of water and soak overnight. Drain and place in a saucepan with plenty of fresh water, bring to the boil, reduce heat and simmer for 1 hour. Drain and keep warm.

To make harissa dressing, mix all ingredients until combined.

Steam or boil broccoli until just tender, then rinse with cold water to stop cooking. ➤

Place couscous in a bowl, pour over 2 cups boiling water, cover and leave to stand for 5 minutes. Stir in butter, using a fork to fluff up the couscous and separate the grains.

Heat oil in a large, non-stick frying pan and sauté onion, garlic, chilli, coriander seeds and ras el hanout over medium heat for 5–6 minutes, stirring occasionally until onion is soft.

Add broccoli and stir until it is heated through and coated with spices. Add cooked chickpeas, couscous, fresh coriander and mint, and pine nuts. Stir until mixed and heated through (keep the heat low so the couscous doesn't stick).

Serve immediately in warmed bowls, garnished with extra coriander and with harissa dressing and yoghurt in separate bowls on the side.

SERVES 4 | VEGAN: SUBSTITUTE SOY YOGHURT FOR NATURAL YOGHURT

Dolmades with pistachios & lemon

250 g vine leaves in brine, drained

¾ cup olive oil

2 onions, finely chopped

¾ cup short grain rice, rinsed

3 spring onions, sliced

¼ teaspoon ground cinnamon

1 clove garlic, crushed

finely grated zest of 1 lemon

2 tablespoons finely chopped fresh dill

2 tablespoons finely chopped fresh mint

60 g chopped unsalted pistachios

salt and freshly ground black pepper

1½ cups vegetable stock

lemon wedges, to serve

Soak vine leaves in warm water for at least 1 hour, rinse and pat dry.

Heat ½ cup of the oil in a large frying pan over low heat. Add onion and sauté for 4–5 minutes until softened but not brown. Add rice, spring onions, cinnamon, garlic, lemon zest, herbs, pistachios, salt and freshly ground pepper. Mix well. Remove from heat.

Lay a vine leaf vein side up on a dry work surface. Place a spoonful of the rice filling near the base of the leaf. Roll the leaf over once, fold in the sides and then roll towards the tip of the leaf. Don't roll it too tightly or when the rice swells the dolma will burst. Continue with more vine leaves until you have used all the filling. >

Line the base of a heavy-based flameproof casserole dish or saucepan with five or six vine leaves. Place the dolmades in, seam-side down, packing them snugly. Pour over remaining oil and place a plate on top to keep them in place. Pour over stock and bring slowly to the boil, then reduce heat, cover and simmer for 45 minutes. Remove plate, then use a slotted spoon to transfer dolmades to a serving dish.

Serve warm or at room temperature, with lemon wedges on the side.

🍄 The number of dolmades made depends on the size of the leaves and the amount of filling. This recipe can make between 20 and 40.

MAKES ABOUT 30 | VEGAN

Felafel

¾ cup chickpeas

1 teaspoon coriander seeds

1 teaspoon cumin seeds

1 onion, roughly chopped

1 clove garlic, chopped

½ cup chopped flat-leaf parsley

pinch of cayenne pepper

salt

vegetable oil, for frying

tahini sauce (page 239), to serve

Put chickpeas in a bowl, cover with plenty of water and soak overnight. Drain and place in a saucepan with plenty of fresh water, bring to the boil, reduce heat and simmer for 1 hour. Drain.

Toast coriander and cumin seeds in a frying pan over high heat for a few minutes – take care as they can burn. Remove from pan, leave to cool then grind with a mortar and pestle or in a grinder.

Place cooked chickpeas, ground seeds, onion, garlic, parsley, cayenne pepper and salt in a blender and blend to form a thick paste. Shape mixture into small balls and press lightly to flatten.

Heat about 2 cm of oil in a large non-stick frying pan over high heat. When oil is hot, shallow-fry the felafel in batches for about 3 minutes on each side or until golden brown and crispy. Drain on paper towel.

Serve with tahini sauce, warmed flatbread and salad.

SERVES 4 | VEGAN

Fennel & cannellini bean stew

150 g dried cannellini beans
(or a 400-g can cannellini
beans, drained and rinsed)

3 tablespoons olive oil

2 cloves garlic, sliced

1 onion, halved and finely sliced

2 leeks, finely sliced

1 × 800-g can chopped tomatoes

1 bay leaf

½ cup chopped flat-leaf parsley

½ cup dry white wine or
vermouth

1 large fennel bulb, trimmed,
halved, cored and sliced

½ cup chopped fresh mint
leaves

salt and freshly ground
black pepper

extra fresh mint leaves, to serve

Place dried cannellini beans in a bowl, cover with plenty of water and soak overnight. Drain and place in a saucepan with plenty of fresh water, bring to the boil, reduce heat and simmer for 50 minutes, or until just tender. Drain and set aside.

Heat oil in a large non-stick frying pan or saucepan, add garlic and onion and sauté for 2–3 minutes. Add leek and sauté for a further 5 minutes, or until softened and starting to brown. Add tomatoes, cooked beans, bay leaf, parsley and wine, bring to the boil and cook for 2–3 minutes. Reduce heat, cover and simmer for about 20 minutes, until sauce has reduced and thickened. ＞

Add fennel, stir and simmer, uncovered, for about 10 minutes, until fennel is cooked (it should still have a little 'crunch'). Stir in mint leaves. Check seasoning and add salt and freshly ground pepper to taste.

To serve, scatter with extra mint leaves.

Don't be tempted to leave out the fresh mint leaves; they make a surprising difference to this dish.

SERVES 6 | VEGAN

French onion pilaf

2 tablespoons olive oil

2 large brown onions, thinly sliced

1 teaspoon ground cardamom

salt and freshly ground black pepper

300 g long grain rice (such as jasmine or basmati), rinsed

3 cups vegetable stock

¼ cup grated parmesan cheese

finely chopped flat-leaf parsley, to serve

Heat oil in a large non-stick frying pan over medium–high heat. Add onion, cardamom, salt and pepper and sauté for 5–6 minutes or until onion starts to soften and brown. Reduce heat, partially cover and cook for about 20 minutes, stirring occasionally, until onion is caramelised.

Add rice and stock to caramelised onions and stir. Bring to the boil, then reduce heat, cover and simmer for 20 minutes. Turn off heat and leave for a few minutes with the lid on.

Add parmesan cheese, check for seasoning and fluff with a fork to separate grains. Serve in warmed bowls, sprinkled with finely chopped parsley.

SERVES 6 | VEGAN: OMIT PARMESAN CHEESE

Lemon & coriander pilaf

2 tablespoons unsalted butter

1 small onion, finely chopped

2 cups basmati rice, rinsed

grated zest of ½ lemon

juice of 1 lemon

1 teaspoon crushed coriander seeds

3 cups water

1 cup milk

2 teaspoons sea salt

2–3 tablespoons chopped fresh coriander leaves, to serve

Melt butter in a medium-sized saucepan over medium heat. Add onion and cook for 3–5 minutes, stirring occasionally, until softened. Add rice and stir until coated. Stir in lemon zest, juice and coriander seeds. Pour in water and bring to the boil. Add milk and salt, stir and bring almost to the boil. Reduce heat, cover and simmer for 15 minutes.

Remove from heat, keep covered and leave to sit for 5 minutes. To serve, fluff rice with a fork and sprinkle with coriander leaves.

SERVES 6

Lentil burgers with coriander mayo

1 × 400-g can brown lentils,
  rinsed and drained

2 cups fresh wholegrain
  breadcrumbs (see note on
  page 59)

1 teaspoon grated fresh ginger

2 teaspoons ground coriander

2 teaspoons ground cumin

1 egg, lightly beaten

salt and freshly ground
  black pepper

¼ cup chopped fresh coriander

2–3 tablespoons plain flour

vegetable oil, for frying

4 bread rolls, halved

2 cups chopped fresh rocket

1 avocado, peeled, stoned
  and cut into long slices

MAYONNAISE

⅓ cup good-quality mayonnaise

1 tablespoon finely chopped
  fresh coriander

2 tablespoons fresh lemon juice

Place lentils, breadcrumbs, ginger, ground coriander and cumin, egg and salt and freshly ground pepper in a blender and pulse until combined but still with some texture. Put into a bowl and stir through fresh coriander until well mixed.

Shape mixture into four round, flat patties and coat each with flour. Chill patties in refrigerator for 10–15 minutes.

Meanwhile, make coriander mayo by mixing mayonnaise, coriander and lemon juice in a small bowl.

Heat oil in a large, non-stick frying pan over medium heat. Cook patties for 3–4 minutes on each side, turning once, until golden brown.

Lightly toast the inside of the bread rolls. Top the four roll bases with rocket, avocado, a lentil pattie and a dollop of mayo, then add the bread roll tops and serve.

SERVES 4

Lentil & vegetable puff pie

2 tablespoons olive oil

1 brown onion, chopped

1 clove garlic, sliced

1 stalk celery, diced

1 carrot, peeled and diced

10 button mushrooms, thickly sliced

1¾ cups green du puy lentils, rinsed

2 tomatoes, peeled and diced

½ cup shelled peas (fresh or frozen)

2 tablespoons chopped flat-leaf parsley

salt and freshly ground black pepper

1 sheet ready-rolled puff pastry

1 egg white, lightly beaten

1 tablespoon sesame seeds

Heat oil in a large saucepan over medium heat. Add onion and garlic and sauté for 1–2 minutes. Add celery, carrot and mushrooms and sauté for a further 2 minutes. Add lentils and enough water to cover. Cover with a lid, bring to the boil, then reduce heat and simmer for 10–15 minutes, until lentils are just tender but still hold their shape. Drain.

Add tomatoes, peas and parsley to lentils, season with salt and freshly ground pepper and leave to cool.

Preheat oven to 200°C. Lightly grease a medium-sized ovenproof pie dish. Defrost pastry.   ＞

Fill prepared dish with cooled lentil mix. Top with pastry, trim to fit and press down edges. Decorate with pastry off-cuts if desired and cut two or three small slits in the pastry. Brush pastry with egg white to glaze and sprinkle with sesame seeds.

Bake for about 30 minutes or until golden.

SERVES 6

Lima beans with rosemary & tomato

500 g lima beans

1 tablespoon olive oil

2 cloves garlic, crushed

1 medium-sized onion,
  finely chopped

3 tablespoons chopped flat-leaf
  parsley

2 small sprigs rosemary

1 × 400-g can crushed tomatoes

salt and freshly ground
  black pepper

finely chopped parsley, to serve

Place beans in a large bowl, cover with plenty of water, soak for 8 hours or overnight, then drain. Put beans in a saucepan, cover with plenty of fresh water and bring to the boil. Boil for 10 minutes, skim any scum from the surface, reduce heat, partially cover and simmer for 1 hour, checking occasionally. When tender, drain and set aside.

Heat oil in a large non-stick saucepan over medium heat, add garlic and onion and sauté, stirring, for 5 minutes or until onion is soft.

Add parsley, rosemary and tomatoes and bring to the boil. Reduce heat, cover and simmer for 20–25 minutes, until sauce thickens. Add cooked beans, season to taste with salt and pepper, then simmer for another 15 minutes. Remove rosemary sprigs.

Serve scattered with parsley, and with plenty of crusty bread.

SERVES 6 | VEGAN

Polenta baked with tomato herb sauce

2 cups water

2 cups vegetable stock

½ teaspoon salt

1 cup polenta

1 tablespoon butter

½ teaspoon ground nutmeg

freshly ground black pepper

SAUCE

1 tablespoon olive oil

1 onion, chopped

1 clove garlic, chopped

1 × 400-g can chopped tomatoes

1 tablespoon tomato paste

1 sprig fresh thyme

salt and freshly ground
   black pepper

½ cup grated mozzarella cheese

½ cup grated parmesan cheese

To make polenta, bring water and vegetable stock to the boil in a large heavy-based non-stick saucepan. Add salt, then slowly pour in polenta, in a fine stream, stirring all the time. Reduce heat and cook for 4–5 minutes, stirring continuously and scraping down the sides of the saucepan. When it is cooked (it should be like a thick porridge, but not grainy) stir in butter, nutmeg and freshly ground pepper.

Lightly grease a 28-cm x 18-cm baking tray or dish with oil. Pour in polenta, smooth the top, cover with cling wrap and leave to set.   ➤

To make tomato herb sauce, heat olive oil in a medium-sized saucepan, add onion and garlic and sauté for 3–4 minutes. Add chopped tomatoes, tomato paste, thyme, salt and freshly ground pepper, cover and simmer for 15–20 minutes.

Preheat oven to 180°C. Lightly oil a medium-sized baking dish.

Cut polenta into 5 cm squares. Put half the polenta squares in the prepared baking dish. Spoon over half the sauce and sprinkle with the mozzarella. Add remaining polenta squares and top with remaining sauce, making sure to cover all of the polenta.

Bake in the oven for 15 minutes. Sprinkle parmesan over the top and bake for a further 10 minutes.

🍄 You can buy polenta at supermarkets or health food stores (where it is often labelled as cornmeal). I recommend using a fine-grained polenta, which cooks more quickly than coarse varieties – if you choose the heavier polenta you will need more liquid and it will need at least 20 minutes of cooking (and stirring).

SERVES 4

Polenta pancakes
with spinach & red capsicum

2 small red capsicums, cut into
  quarters lengthways and
  deseeded

1 cup milk

½ cup fresh lemon juice

1 egg, lightly beaten

¾ cup self-raising flour

½ teaspoon baking powder

½ teaspoon salt

½ cup polenta
  (see note on page 132)

olive oil, for frying

50 g unsalted butter

1 cup baby spinach leaves,
  stalks removed

1 tablespoon capers

Preheat oven to 200°C.

Brush capsicums lightly with oil. Place on a non-stick oven tray and roast
for 25–30 minutes, turning once or twice, until soft and slightly charred at
the edges. Remove from oven, place in a bowl, cover with cling wrap and
set aside for 10 minutes (the trapped steam will make it easier to peel off
the skins). Remove skins and slice capsicums into long strips.

Place milk, half the lemon juice and the egg in a small bowl and mix. Sift
flour, baking powder and salt into a large bowl, then stir in polenta. Pour in
milk mixture and whisk until combined. Set aside for 30 minutes. >

Heat oil in a non-stick frying pan over medium heat. When the pan is hot, spoon in tablespoons of the polenta batter and cook for a few minutes on each side until golden. Transfer pancakes to a warmed plate and keep in the oven until all pancakes are cooked.

Heat remaining lemon juice in a small saucepan over medium heat. Whisk in butter until combined.

To serve, arrange two pancakes on each plate, top with some spinach leaves, capsicum strips and capers and drizzle with the warm lemon butter sauce. Serve immediately.

SERVES 4

Red dahl

3 tablespoons vegetable oil

2 brown onions, finely sliced

2 cloves garlic, crushed

2-cm piece fresh ginger, grated

1 teaspoon ground cumin

1 teaspoon ground turmeric

300 g red lentils, rinsed

2 cups water

1 teaspoon garam masala

salt

2 tablespoons fresh lime juice

fresh coriander leaves, to serve

Heat oil in a non-stick saucepan over medium heat. Add onion and garlic and sauté for 2–3 minutes until golden. Add ginger, cumin and turmeric and continue cooking for a few minutes until fragrance is released.

Add lentils to the pan with the onions and stir to coat with oil and spices. Add water, bring to the boil, then reduce heat, cover and simmer for about 15 minutes. The dahl should be of a thick, porridge-like consistency – if dahl becomes too dry, add a little more boiling water. Stir in garam masala, salt to taste and lime juice.

Serve garnished with coriander leaves.

🍄 Dahl is traditionally served in India with rice, flatbreads or chapatti. It is high in protein, especially when served with a grain such as rice.

SERVES 4–6 | VEGAN

Roasted pumpkin & sage risotto

1 butternut pumpkin, peeled
and cut into 2-cm cubes

¼ cup olive oil

salt and freshly ground
black pepper

2 tablespoons butter

2 cloves garlic, crushed

1¼ cups risotto rice
(such as Arborio)

generous pinch of ground
nutmeg

12 fresh sage leaves

5 cups hot vegetable stock

200 ml dry white wine (or use
extra stock)

½ cup grated parmesan cheese

salt and freshly ground
black pepper

extra fresh sage leaves, to serve

Preheat oven to 200°C.

Put pumpkin on a non-stick baking tray, brush with a little olive oil and sprinkle with salt and pepper. Roast for 20–25 minutes until tender.

Heat remaining olive oil and butter in a medium-sized heavy-based saucepan over medium heat. When butter starts to sizzle, add garlic and sauté for 1 minute. Add rice, nutmeg and sage leaves, stir until rice is coated, then pour in a ladleful of hot stock. Stir until almost all liquid is absorbed. Add wine and stir until liquid is absorbed. Pour in remaining hot stock, stir well, cover, reduce heat to very low and cook for about 15–16 minutes, stirring occasionally. >

When all liquid is absorbed, test the rice – it should be al dente (soft but still with a little 'bite' to it). If it is not cooked, add a tiny bit of extra stock or boiling water, and stir until it is absorbed.

When rice is cooked, stir in roasted pumpkin and parmesan cheese. Check seasoning and add salt and pepper if needed.

Serve immediately in warmed bowls with a twist of ground pepper and a sprinkling of fresh sage leaves.

Traditionally, a risotto is made by adding the hot stock a ladleful at a time, stirring constantly, and adding more stock only when the liquid is almost all absorbed. I find that once the rice has absorbed some of the liquid, you can achieve a similar creamy result by adding the remaining stock, covering the pot and stirring only occasionally.

SERVES 4

Soft polenta with mushroom ragout

3 tablespoons olive oil

3 cloves garlic, crushed

200 g mixed mushrooms
(e.g. shiitake, oyster, Swiss
brown), thinly sliced

350 g button mushrooms,
thinly sliced

1½ cups passata (tomato purée)

½ cup red wine (optional)

1 sprig fresh thyme

salt and freshly ground
black pepper

grated parmesan cheese, to serve
(optional)

POLENTA

2 cups water

1 cup vegetable stock

1 cup milk

½ teaspoon salt

1 cup polenta (see note on
page 132)

1 tablespoon butter

freshly ground black pepper

To make ragout, heat oil over medium heat in a medium-sized heavy-based saucepan. Add garlic and cook for 1–2 minutes. Add mushrooms and sauté, stirring, for 6–7 minutes or until softened. Add passata, red wine (if using), thyme, salt and freshly ground pepper. Stir, then partially cover and simmer for about 15 minutes until sauce thickens and reduces.

To make polenta, bring water, vegetable stock and milk to the boil in a large, non-stick saucepan. Add salt, then slowly pour in polenta, in a fine stream, stirring all the time. Reduce heat and cook for 4–5 minutes, stirring continuously and scraping down the sides of the saucepan. >

When polenta is cooked (it should be like a thick porridge, but not grainy) stir in butter and freshly ground pepper.

As soon as polenta is cooked, spoon into warmed bowls and top with mushroom ragout. Sprinkle over grated parmesan cheese if desired and serve immediately.

SERVES 4 | VEGAN: OMIT BUTTER AND PARMESAN CHEESE

Spiced chickpeas & broad beans

500 g shelled broad beans (fresh or frozen)

1 × 400-g can chickpeas, drained and rinsed (or 150 g dried chickpeas, cooked – see pages 92–93)

½ cup shelled peas (fresh or frozen)

1 red onion, finely sliced

1 small red chilli, deseeded and finely sliced

1 tablespoon sweet paprika

1 tablespoon ground cumin

½ cup chopped fresh coriander

1 tablespoon chopped fresh mint leaves

naan bread, to serve

DRESSING

1 clove garlic, crushed

¼ cup olive oil

1 tablespoon soy sauce

If using fresh broad beans, cook in boiling water for 4–5 minutes until tender. Drain, then remove outer pod by popping it off between your finger and thumb. If beans are frozen, place them in a bowl, cover with boiling water and leave for 1 minute. Drain, then remove outer pod.

Place all salad ingredients in a large bowl and toss to combine.

To make dressing, whisk together garlic, oil and soy sauce. Pour dressing over bean mixture and toss. Serve at room temperature with warm naan bread.

SERVES 4 | VEGAN

Tortillas with Mexican beans

1 tablespoon olive oil

1 onion, chopped

1 clove garlic, chopped

½ green capsicum, diced

1 small red chilli, deseeded
and finely sliced

1 × 400-g can chopped tomatoes

1 × 400-g can red kidney beans,
drained and rinsed (or 150 g
dried red kidney beans,
cooked – see pages 92–93)

salt and freshly ground
black pepper

4 flour tortillas

1 avocado, peeled, stoned and
cut into small cubes

1 cup natural yoghurt

1 cup chopped fresh coriander

Heat oil in a large saucepan over medium heat. Add onion and sauté
for 3–4 minutes, add garlic and green capsicum and fry for a further
5 minutes. Add chilli and tomatoes, bring to the boil, then reduce heat
and simmer, uncovered, for 15 minutes, until sauce thickens and reduces.

Stir in kidney beans and cook until heated through. The sauce should be
quite thick, with tomato sauce just coating the beans. Season with salt
and freshly ground pepper to taste.   >

Heat tortillas under a preheated grill or wrap in aluminium foil and place in a 180°C preheated oven for 10 minutes.

To serve, top each warmed tortilla with a scoop of bean mix, some avocado, a dollop of yoghurt and plenty of coriander. Serve immediately.

SERVES 4 | VEGAN: SUBSTITUTE SOY YOGHURT FOR NATURAL YOGHURT

Warm broad beans
with radicchio & pecorino

125 g shelled broad beans (fresh or frozen)

2 tablespoons olive oil

3 cloves garlic, finely chopped

salt and freshly ground black pepper

3 cups shredded radicchio

¼ cup vinaigrette (page 242)

100 g pecorino cheese, shaved (or use parmesan)

1 tablespoon chopped fresh mint leaves

If using fresh broad beans, cook in boiling water for 4–5 minutes until tender. Drain, then remove outer pod by popping it off between your finger and thumb. If beans are frozen, place them in a bowl, cover with boiling water and leave for 1 minute. Drain, then remove outer pod.

Heat oil in a non-stick frying pan over medium heat, add garlic and sauté for 2–3 minutes. Add beans and cook, stirring, until coated with oil and heated through. Season with salt and freshly ground pepper.

Pile radicchio onto four plates. Spoon broad beans on top, drizzle with vinaigrette, scatter with shaved pecorino and mint and serve.

SERVES 4

Warm red lentils with coriander & currants

2 tablespoons olive oil
1 clove garlic, sliced
1 onion, halved and thinly sliced
1 teaspoon grated fresh ginger
1 teaspoon grated lemon zest
2 teaspoons cumin seeds
1 teaspoon ground coriander
1 cup red lentils, rinsed

2 tablespoons fresh lemon juice
2 cups vegetable stock
½ cup currants
½ cup fresh coriander leaves
salt and freshly ground
  black pepper
lemon wedges, to serve

Heat olive oil in a large non-stick frying pan over medium heat. Add garlic, onion, ginger, lemon zest, cumin seeds and ground coriander. Sauté for 2–3 minutes until onion is soft. Add lentils and stir until coated with spices.

Add lemon juice and 1 cup of the stock, stir and simmer for about 5 minutes until liquid is absorbed. Add remaining stock and currants, cover and simmer for about 5 minutes until lentils are soft and liquid is absorbed (lentils should hold their shape – don't overcook or they will become mushy). Remove from heat and leave to stand for a few minutes. Add coriander leaves, reserving a few for garnish, season with salt and pepper and stir gently. Serve with coriander leaves sprinkled on top and lemon wedges on the side.

SERVES 4 | VEGAN

Salads

A salad can be a simple bowl of peppery rocket with a drizzle of the finest extra virgin olive oil, or it can be a wonderful coming together of golden chickpeas tossed with roasted vegetables, nuts and seeds — a colourful, filling, nourishing meal.

Although salad leaves are about 90 per cent water they also contain antioxidants, minerals, and vitamins including vitamin C and folate. Choose the freshest salad greens and store them carefully to keep them that way. Or why not try growing your own? Always wash salad greens carefully before using, and dry them thoroughly using a salad spinner (otherwise the dressing won't coat the leaves).

Try different herbs in your salads and experiment with dressings and oils. Add seeds and nuts for extra crunch and additional nutrition.

‹ Almost Niçoise salad (page 150)

Almost Niçoise salad

450 g small chat or waxy potatoes

250 g baby green beans,
   topped and tailed

4 cups mixed salad leaves
   or 1 butter lettuce torn
   into pieces

200 g cherry tomatoes, halved

4 hard-boiled eggs, shelled
   and quartered

100 g small black olives

¼ cup chopped fresh chives

salt and freshly ground
   black pepper

⅓ cup vinaigrette (page 242)

Steam or boil potatoes until just tender. Drain.

Bring about 3 cm of water to the boil in a saucepan, toss in green beans, cover and cook for 2–3 minutes, until just tender but still bright green. Drain, dip into ice-cold water to stop them cooking and drain again.

Arrange salad greens on a large platter or individual plates. Arrange warm potatoes, tomatoes, green beans, egg pieces and olives on top. Sprinkle with chives, season with salt and freshly ground pepper, and drizzle with dressing. Serve immediately.

A traditional Niçoise salad has tuna and sometimes anchovies, but this combination of vegetables and sharp French dressing is just as irresistible without them.

SERVES 4

Baby greens with pear & toasted hazelnuts

1 firm pear

3 cups mixed baby green salad leaves

75 g hazelnuts, toasted and chopped

DRESSING

3 tablespoons olive oil

1 tablespoon hazelnut or walnut oil

1 tablespoon white wine vinegar

1 teaspoon Dijon mustard

salt

To make hazelnut dressing, place all ingredients in a small screw-top jar and shake until combined, or whisk ingredients in a small bowl.

Just before serving, quarter and core the pear (leave the skin on) and cut into thin slices. Place salad leaves in a large bowl. Add pear slices and hazelnuts, pour over dressing, toss and serve immediately.

SERVES 4 | VEGAN

Beetroot, fetta & spinach salad

12 baby beetroots, scrubbed

4 cups baby spinach leaves, stalks removed

150 g fetta, crumbled into chunks

2 tablespoons finely chopped spring onions

2 tablespoons chopped fresh mint

1 cup walnuts, toasted

⅓ cup vinaigrette (page 242)

salt and freshly ground black pepper

Leave top and root of beetroots intact, place in boiling water, cover and simmer gently for 45–50 minutes, or until tender. When cool, rub skins off (wear rubber gloves to avoid staining your fingers), remove tops and roots and slice in half.

Divide spinach leaves between serving plates. Arrange beetroot halves on top of spinach and scatter over fetta, spring onions, mint and walnuts. Pour dressing over the salad and season with salt and a good twist of freshly ground pepper.

SERVES 4

Black bean salad

250 g black beans

4 spring onions, sliced

12 cherry tomatoes, halved

1 cup sweet corn kernels (fresh or frozen)

1 avocado, peeled, stoned and cut into 1-cm cubes

½ cup chopped fresh coriander

salt and freshly ground black pepper

rocket leaves, to serve

small handful torn fresh basil leaves, to serve

DRESSING

¼ cup extra virgin olive oil

2 tablespoons fresh lemon juice

1 clove garlic, crushed

pinch of cayenne pepper

Put black beans in a bowl, cover with plenty of cold water and soak overnight. Drain, put beans in a saucepan, cover with plenty of fresh water, bring to the boil and boil for about 10 minutes. Reduce heat, partially cover and simmer for 1½–2 hours until beans are tender. Drain and cool.

To make lemon dressing, put all ingredients in a small screw-top jar and shake well.

In a large bowl combine cooked beans, spring onions, tomatoes, sweet corn, avocado and coriander. Add lemon dressing and toss well. Season with salt and freshly ground pepper to taste.

To serve, arrange rocket leaves on a serving platter, spoon bean mix over the rocket and scatter basil leaves on top.

Black beans (sometimes called turtle beans or black kidney beans) take a long time to cook, but they have their own unusual flavour and are worth trying. They are also high in fibre and vegetable protein. It is unusual to see them in cans in Australia, but they are sometimes available from specialist food suppliers.

SERVES 4–6 | VEGAN

Cabbage, carrot & seed salad

2 carrots, peeled and grated

½ small cabbage, finely
  shredded

2 tablespoons sesame seeds,
  toasted

1 tablespoon poppy seeds

salt and freshly ground
  black pepper

2 tablespoons chopped
  fresh chives

DRESSING

3 tablespoons olive oil

2 tablespoons fresh lemon juice

2 tablespoons natural yoghurt

½ teaspoon mustard powder

To make dressing, place all ingredients in a small screw-top jar and shake until well combined. Refrigerate until ready to use.

To make salad, put grated carrot, cabbage, and sesame and poppy seeds in a serving bowl and toss to combine. Pour over dressing and toss lightly. Check for seasoning and add salt and pepper if needed. Sprinkle with chopped chives and serve.

SERVES 4–6 | VEGAN: SUBSTITUTE SOY YOGHURT FOR NATURAL YOGHURT

Chickpea salad
with cumin-seed dressing

2 × 400-g cans chickpeas,
  drained and rinsed (or 360 g
  dried chickpeas, cooked – see
  pages 92–93)

1 cup roasted red capsicum,
  diced

2 spring onions, sliced

200 g cherry tomatoes, halved

1 cup roughly chopped flat-leaf
  parsley

salt and freshly ground
  black pepper

DRESSING

1 tablespoon cumin seeds

½ cup extra virgin olive oil

3 tablespoons white balsamic
  vinegar

salt and freshly ground
  black pepper

To make cumin-seed dressing, heat a frying pan over medium heat then add cumin seeds and toast until they start to pop and release their fragrance. Place 2 teaspoons of the toasted seeds in a mortar and pestle (reserving the remainder) and crush. Put olive oil, balsamic vinegar, salt and freshly ground pepper in a small bowl and whisk until the mixture emulsifies, then stir in the ground cumin.

Place cooked chickpeas in a saucepan, cover with cold water and bring to the boil. Cook for about 2 minutes until heated through. Drain and place in a large bowl. While still warm stir in diced red capsicum, spring onions, cherry tomatoes and parsley. Season with salt and pepper and mix well.

Pour the dressing over the salad, add reserved toasted cumin seeds and toss well. Serve at room temperature.

🍄 You can buy roasted red capsicums from most delis, or you can roast them yourself (see page 235).

SERVES 4–6 | VEGAN

Fattoush salad

1 large pita bread (or 2 small pita bread pockets)

3 tomatoes, chopped

3 Lebanese cucumbers, cut into thick slices

1 red capsicum, halved, deseeded and cut into rings

1 red onion, thinly sliced

½ cup wild rocket

½ cup torn baby cos lettuce leaves

½ cup chopped flat-leaf parsley

½ cup chopped fresh mint leaves

DRESSING

5 tablespoons olive oil

3 tablespoons fresh lemon juice

1 clove garlic, crushed

1 tablespoon sumac

salt and freshly ground black pepper

Split pita bread open, toast until golden then break into bite-sized pieces.

To make dressing, whisk together oil, lemon juice, garlic, sumac, and salt and pepper.

To make the salad, place tomatoes, cucumber, red capsicum, onion, rocket, cos lettuce, parsley and mint leaves into a large bowl and toss to combine. Pour dressing over salad and just before serving toss through the crisp bread, reserving a few pieces for the top.

SERVES 4–6 | VEGAN

Gado gado

12 small waxy or chat potatoes

200 g green beans, topped
and tailed

200 g bean sprouts

1 baby cos lettuce, trimmed

2 Lebanese cucumbers,
thickly sliced

6 hard-boiled eggs, shelled
and quartered

SATAY SAUCE

2 tablespoons peanut oil

½ red onion, diced

1 red chilli, deseeded
and finely sliced

2 cloves garlic, chopped

1 tablespoon grated fresh ginger

1 × 400-ml can coconut milk

6 tablespoons crunchy peanut
butter

1 tablespoon tamari or dark soy

1 teaspoon soft brown sugar

2 tablespoons fresh lemon juice

salt

To make satay sauce, heat peanut oil in a small saucepan over medium heat. Add onion, chilli, garlic and ginger and sauté for 7–8 minutes until onion is quite soft. Add coconut milk, peanut butter, tamari, sugar and lemon juice and simmer over low heat for 10 minutes, until the sauce thickens. Test for seasoning and add salt if desired.

Steam or boil the potatoes until just tender.   ❯

Steam or boil the green beans for 2–3 minutes, then rinse under cold water to stop them cooking. Slice on an angle into bite-sized pieces. Pour boiling water over bean sprouts, then rinse in cold water.

Spread cos leaves over a platter, arrange potatoes, cucumber, green beans, bean sprouts and egg pieces on top. Pour over some warm peanut sauce and serve with extra sauce on the side.

This Indonesian salad can vary enormously, but potatoes, eggs, peanut sauce and crispy kropuk or prawn crackers are traditional ingredients. Non-vegetarians might like to add prawn crackers. Puffed fried tofu can also be added.

SERVES 6 | VEGAN

Insalata caprese

4 vine-ripened tomatoes
8 fresh bocconcini (mozzarella balls)
fresh basil leaves
extra virgin olive oil
salt and freshly ground black pepper

Cut tomatoes and bocconcini into thick slices. Arrange slices on a platter, alternating tomato, mozzarella and basil leaves. Drizzle with olive oil and sprinkle with salt and freshly ground pepper.

Make sure you buy the fresh soft white mozzarella that is usually packed in brine (not the harder yellow mozzarella used for pizza topping). Although rather extravagant, if you can find really fresh soft buffalo mozzarella it makes this salad into a Roman feast. Remember to store your tomatoes at room temperature for maximum flavour.

SERVES 4

Japanese spinach & pickled ginger salad

200 g baby spinach leaves, stalks removed

2 sheets nori seaweed, cut into strips

1 Lebanese cucumber, cut into small sticks

4–5 small pieces pickled ginger

2 tablespoons sesame seeds, toasted

DRESSING

2 tablespoons rice wine vinegar

2 tablespoons sesame oil

1 tablespoon olive oil

1 tablespoon tamari

½ teaspoon sugar

To make dressing, place all ingredients in a small screw-top jar and shake to combine, or mix in a small bowl.

To make salad, place spinach leaves in a serving bowl, add seaweed and cucumber. Pour the dressing over and toss lightly. Arrange pickled ginger on top and scatter with sesame seeds.

SERVES 4 | VEGAN

Lentil salad with lemon & mint

300 g green du puy lentils

1 red onion, halved

1 cinnamon stick

2 cloves

a small piece lemon zest

1 clove garlic, finely sliced

1 teaspoon ground coriander

1 teaspoon ground cumin

3 tablespoons chopped fresh
  mint

2 springs onions, finely sliced

DRESSING

3 tablespoons extra virgin
  olive oil

3 tablespoons fresh lemon juice

salt

Place lentils, onion, cinnamon stick, cloves, lemon zest, garlic and spices in a medium-sized saucepan and cover with water. Bring to the boil, skim off any scum, then simmer over medium heat for 25–30 minutes until water is absorbed. Remove onion, cinnamon stick and lemon zest.

To make the dressing, whisk together the oil, lemon juice and salt.

Place lentils in a serving bowl, stir through fresh mint and spring onions, pour dressing over the salad and toss to coat.

Serve at room temperature.

SERVES 4–6 | VEGAN

Moroccan carrot salad

500 g carrots, peeled and
  coarsely grated

¼ cup currants

½ cup chopped fresh coriander

¼ cup chopped pistachios,
  to serve

DRESSING

1 teaspoon cumin seeds

3 cardamom pods, crushed

3 tablespoons fresh lemon juice

3 tablespoons olive oil

1 small clove garlic, crushed

1 teaspoon sweet paprika

salt

To make the dressing, place cumin seeds and crushed cardamom pods in a frying pan over medium heat and cook for about 1 minute until seeds start to pop and fragrance is released. Leave to cool for a few minutes then discard the cardamom pods. Crush seeds with a mortar and pestle, or in a grinder. Place lemon juice, oil, garlic, paprika, salt and crushed seeds in a small screw-top jar and shake until well mixed.

To make the salad, place grated carrots, currants and coriander in a bowl. Pour dressing over the salad and toss to combine. Cover and leave for at least two hours to allow flavours to develop.

When ready to serve, pile salad onto a serving dish and sprinkle with pistachios.

SERVES 4–6 | VEGAN

Roast pumpkin & green bean salad

1 kg pumpkin, peeled and cut
   into 2.5-cm cubes

2 tablespoons olive oil

1 tablespoon ground cumin

200 g green beans, topped
   and tailed

100 g rocket

100 g fetta, cut into small cubes

¾ cup slivered almonds, toasted

salt and freshly ground
   black pepper

DRESSING

3 tablespoons vegetable oil

1 tablespoon sesame oil

1 tablespoon tamari

salt and freshly ground
   black pepper

Preheat oven to 200°C.

Place pumpkin in a roasting pan, drizzle with olive oil, sprinkle with cumin and toss to combine. Roast for 20–25 minutes, turning occasionally, until pumpkin is soft and slightly darkened around the edges.

To make the dressing, place all ingredients in a small screw-top jar and shake well, or mix in a small bowl.

Bring some water to the boil in a medium-sized saucepan. Add green beans and cook for 3 minutes. Drain and place in iced water for 1 minute to stop cooking, then drain again. **>**

Place rocket on a platter or in a serving bowl, and arrange pumpkin, fetta, green beans and toasted almonds on top. Pour dressing over and toss to combine. Season with salt and freshly ground black pepper.

SERVES 4

Spinach, fetta & orange salad

1 orange

150 g baby spinach leaves, stalks removed

150 g soft fetta, cut into small cubes

16 pitted kalamata olives

2 tablespoons finely chopped flat-leaf parsley

DRESSING

2 tablespoons cider vinegar

½ teaspoon Dijon mustard

1 clove garlic, crushed

⅓ cup fruity virgin olive oil

salt and freshly ground black pepper

To make dressing, place all ingredients in a small screw-top jar and shake until blended, or mix in a small bowl.

To make the salad, peel the orange, remove all pith and carefully divide into segments. Place spinach leaves in a large serving bowl. Add fetta, orange segments and olives. Pour over just enough dressing to lightly coat the spinach leaves, toss gently, sprinkle with parsley and serve.

🍄 If you prefer, you can divide the salad among individual plates and arrange orange, fetta and olives on top of the leaves, then pour the dressing over.

SERVES 4

Tabbouleh

½ cup burghul (cracked wheat)

4 spring onions, finely chopped

1 Lebanese cucumber, diced

3 tomatoes, deseeded and diced

1½ cups finely chopped flat-leaf parsley

2 tablespoons finely chopped fresh mint leaves

DRESSING

juice of 1 lemon

1 clove garlic, crushed

3 tablespoons olive oil

salt and freshly ground black pepper

Put burghul in a bowl and cover with boiling water. Cover and set aside for 15 minutes. Drain and press out as much water as possible from the wheat.

To make dressing, place all ingredients in a small screw-top jar and shake until combined, or whisk together in a small bowl.

Combine burghul, spring onions, cucumber, tomato and herbs in a serving bowl, pour the dressing over and toss to combine.

SERVES 4 | VEGAN

Thai salad with hot & sour dressing

½ cup fresh Vietnamese
  mint leaves

½ cup fresh coriander leaves

10 fresh Thai basil leaves

1 fennel bulb, trimmed and
  sliced into thin strips

2 spring onions, sliced
  on an angle

1 long red chilli, finely sliced

1 green chilli, finely sliced

2 red shallots, finely sliced

2 cups shredded Chinese
  cabbage

1 cup bean sprouts, ends
  trimmed

½ cup chopped unsalted
  roasted peanuts

DRESSING

¼ cup fresh lime juice

1 teaspoon sesame oil

3 tablespoons tamarind juice

2 teaspoons caster sugar

3 tablespoons light soy sauce

a few thin slices red chilli

To make the hot and sour dressing, place all ingredients in a small
screw-top jar and shake well, or mix in a small bowl.

Pile all salad ingredients, except peanuts, onto a platter. Pour the
dressing over and toss well. Sprinkle peanuts over the top and serve.

SERVES 4 | VEGAN

Tortellini salad with asparagus, red capsicum & pine nuts

12 asparagus spears, trimmed

500 g cheese tortellini

1 red capsicum, deseeded and
cut into long thin strips

½ cup pine nuts, toasted

2 tablespoons finely chopped
flat-leaf parsley

DRESSING

⅓ cup olive oil

3 tablespoons fresh lemon juice

1 clove garlic, crushed

salt and freshly ground
black pepper

To make dressing, combine ingredients in a small screw-top jar and shake well, or mix together in small bowl.

Lightly steam or boil the asparagus until cooked but still firm (it will take about 5 minutes to boil, and slightly longer to steam, depending on the thickness of the spears). Drain and plunge into iced water for a minute or two to stop them cooking. Drain well, then cut each spear into three or four pieces.

Cook tortellini in plenty of salted boiling water according to packet instructions until al dente (be careful not to overcook it or the salad will be soggy). Drain, rinse quickly under cold water to stop cooking, then drain well. >

Tip tortellini into a large bowl. Add cooked asparagus and red capsicum strips, pour the dressing over and toss lightly. Cover and leave for at least 30 minutes to allow flavours to develop.

To serve, toss again and scatter toasted pine nuts and chopped parsley over the top. (If the salad seems a little dry, add an extra squeeze of lemon juice.)

🍄 Choose asparagus spears of the same thickness so that they cook in the same amount time. To trim, snap off the ends – the spears will break just above the woody base.

SERVES 4

Wild rice salad with cashews

1 cinnamon stick

½ cup wild rice, rinsed

1 cup long grain brown rice, rinsed

1 spring onion, finely sliced

1 red capsicum, deseeded and diced

1 cup grated carrot

1 tablespoon grated fresh ginger

¼ cup chopped roasted cashews

freshly ground black pepper

DRESSING

¼ cup olive oil

2 tablespoons fresh lemon juice

1 tablespoon rice wine vinegar

1 tablespoon tamari

2 tablespoons sesame seeds, toasted

Bring a large saucepan of water to the boil, add cinnamon stick, wild rice and brown rice and boil for 15 minutes or until rice is cooked. Drain, rinse and drain again. Return to pan, cover and leave for 5 minutes. Fluff with a fork and allow to cool.

To make the sesame dressing, place all ingredients in a small screw-top jar and shake to combine, or mix in a small bowl.

Place cooked rice, spring onion, capsicum, carrot, ginger and cashews in a serving bowl, add sesame dressing and toss well. Check for seasoning and add pepper if needed. Serve at room temperature.

SERVES 6 | VEGAN

Winter fennel salad

2 tablespoons olive oil

2 tablespoons brown
mustard seeds

3 carrots, peeled and cut into
long thin strips

1 leek, cut into long thin strips

1 fennel bulb, trimmed, halved
and cut into thin strips

1 tablespoon sesame seeds,
toasted

finely grated zest of 1 orange

DRESSING

3 tablespoons olive oil

1 tablespoon cider vinegar

1 teaspoon Dijon mustard

salt

To make dressing, whisk all ingredients together until creamy.

To make salad, heat 1 tablespoon olive oil in a frying pan, add mustard seeds and cook for 1–2 minutes, until the seeds start to pop. Add remaining olive oil, carrots and leek and sauté for 1 minute. Stir in fennel and sauté for another minute. Add sesame seeds and stir through grated orange zest. Transfer to a bowl, add dressing and toss while still warm.

The secret to this salad is to cut all the vegetables into long, thin, even strips – a mandoline does the job perfectly.

SERVES 4 | VEGAN

Vegetable dishes

Vegetables are an essential part of any diet, but particularly a vegetarian diet. In Australia, the influence of multi-culturalism means ingredients such as fresh Italian porcini mushrooms and Chinese bok choy are standard vegetable fare, available even in supermarkets. But while super-markets do offer abundance, whenever possible try to shop at a specialist greengrocer, wholefoods supplier or farmer's market — the seasonal, organic and fresh produce you'll find provides better nutritional value and flavour.

Variety is important, so consume a range of vegetables: roots and tubers such as carrots and beetroot; brassicas and leafy vegetables like broccoli, cauliflower and spinach; shoot vegetables including asparagus and fennel; vegetable fruits (botanically speaking) such as tomatoes and eggplant; and pods and seeds such as peas, sweet corn and broad beans. There are innumerable options, so eat up those vegetables!

< Baked eggplant & ricotta rolls (page 184)

Baked eggplant & ricotta rolls

2 large elongated eggplants
(400–500 g in total)

⅓ cup olive oil

2 cups passata (tomato purée)

250 g ricotta

½ cup grated mozzarella

¾ cup grated parmesan cheese

⅓ cup currants

½ cup chopped flat-leaf parsley

salt and freshly ground
black pepper

½ cup fresh multigrain
breadcrumbs (see note on
page 59)

extra chopped flat-leaf parsley,
to serve

Cut eggplants lengthways into slices about 1 cm thick. Heat half the olive oil in a large non-stick frying pan and fry half the eggplant slices for 2–3 minutes or until lightly brown on each side. Remove and drain on paper towel. Add the rest of the oil to the pan and fry the remaining eggplant. The eggplant will absorb quite a lot of oil, but keep turning the pieces rather than adding extra oil; if they are a little charred it adds to the flavour.

Preheat oven to 180°C. Spread ½ cup passata over the bottom of a medium-sized ovenproof baking dish.

Place ricotta, mozzarella, ½ cup parmesan cheese, currants, half the parsley, salt and a good twist of black pepper in a bowl and mix together.

Place a tablespoon of the ricotta mix onto each eggplant slice and roll up firmly. Place eggplant rolls into the baking dish, seam-side down, fitted snugly together in a single layer. Pour remaining passata over the top, making sure to cover all the rolls.

Combine remaining parmesan, parsley and breadcrumbs and scatter over the rolls. Cover with aluminium foil and bake for 25 minutes. Remove foil and bake for about 10 minutes until cheese is melted and top is crusty.

Sprinkle over extra parsley and serve.

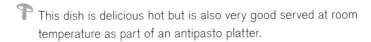 This dish is delicious hot but is also very good served at room temperature as part of an antipasto platter.

SERVES 6

Caramelised onion tart

2 tablespoons olive oil

1 kg brown onions, finely sliced

1 tablespoon balsamic vinegar

1 tablespoon soft brown sugar

1 sheet ready-rolled puff pastry

½ cup grated parmesan cheese

2 large eggs

salt and freshly ground black pepper

Heat oil in a large heavy-based frying pan over medium heat, add onions and sauté, stirring, for 5–6 minutes until the onions begin to soften and change colour. Add balsamic vinegar and sugar and stir. Reduce heat, partially cover, and cook for 35–40 minutes, stirring occasionally, until onions are dark brown and caramelised. Cool to room temperature.

Preheat oven to 200°C. Lightly grease a 35-cm × 12-cm non-stick loose-bottomed tart dish. Defrost pastry.

Cut pastry to fit the tart dish, trimming off any excess. Cover and refrigerate for 10 minutes. Remove pastry-lined dish from refrigerator, sprinkle parmesan over the base and spoon in the onion mixture.   >

Lightly beat eggs with salt and freshly ground pepper, then pour into the dish to cover the onions. Bake in the oven for 30–35 minutes (check after 20 minutes – if the pastry is getting too dark, cover with aluminium foil).

Remove from oven and leave to cool until just warm before serving.

SERVES 6

Eggplant & coconut spiked with chilli

2 tablespoons sesame oil

1 red onion, chopped

2 cloves garlic, crushed

2 large eggplants
   (about 360–400 g in total),
   cut into 3-cm cubes

1 small red bird's-eye chilli,
   deseeded and sliced

1 cup coconut milk

1 cup water

salt and freshly ground
   black pepper

1 cup chopped fresh coriander

steamed jasmine rice, to serve

Heat oil in a frying pan over medium heat. Add onion and garlic and sauté for 4–5 minutes until softened. Add eggplant and chilli to the pan and cook, stirring, for about 5 minutes. Stir in coconut milk and water, bring to the boil, then reduce heat, cover and simmer for 20 minutes until eggplant is soft and sauce is reduced. If there is too much liquid, remove lid, increase heat and cook for a few minutes until sauce thickens and reduces.

Check seasoning and add salt and freshly ground pepper if necessary. Stir through coriander and serve with steamed jasmine rice.

🍄 Refrigerate this dish overnight to allow the flavours to really develop. It can be eaten hot or at room temperature.

SERVES 4

Mushrooms baked with pesto

6 very large field mushrooms

¾ cup pesto (page 233)

100 g ricotta

Preheat oven to 180°C.

Wipe mushrooms clean and cut away entire stem.

Spoon pesto into the centre of each mushroom and spread over. Add a scoop of ricotta to each mushroom and spread to cover the surface.

Bake in the oven for 15 minutes.

🍄 This makes a terrific, easy Sunday night meal when served with grilled tomatoes, a big green salad and crusty bread. Use goat's cheese if you prefer, and for a change try using roasted red capsicum and walnut dip (page 235) instead of basil pesto.

SERVES 6 (AS A LIGHT MEAL OR SIDE DISH)

Potato & corn fritters
with roasted cherry tomatoes

8 cherry tomatoes

500 g floury potatoes, peeled
 and chopped

2 eggs, separated

¼ cup self-raising flour

½ cup warm milk

1 cup sweet corn kernels
 (fresh or frozen)

salt

5–6 fresh mint leaves, chopped

olive or sunflower oil, for frying

1 cup watercress

½ cup crème fraîche or natural
 yoghurt

freshly ground black pepper

Preheat oven to 170°C.

Place tomatoes on a non-stick baking tray and roast for 20 minutes.

Boil or steam potatoes for 15–20 minutes, until tender. Drain well and mash.
Stir in egg yolks, sifted flour, milk, corn, salt and mint. Whisk egg whites
in a clean bowl until stiff peaks form, then gradually fold into potato mixture.

Heat oil in a non-stick frying pan, add spoonfuls of the potato batter and
cook for 3–4 minutes on each side, turning once, until golden brown.
Keep cooked fritters warm in the oven until all mixture has been used.

Place fritters on warmed plates, top with watercress, tomatoes and a
spoonful of crème fraîche or yoghurt, then season with pepper and serve.

SERVES 4

Potato, fetta & chive cakes

500 g potatoes
120 g fetta, crumbled
½ cup chopped fresh chives
1 egg, lightly beaten
1 teaspoon grated lemon zest
1 tablespoon fresh lemon juice
freshly ground black pepper
flour, for coating
3 tablespoons olive oil

Steam or boil potatoes until tender, then place in a large bowl and mash.
Add fetta, chives, egg, lemon zest and juice, and plenty of freshly ground
pepper. Mix to combine, then cover and refrigerate for 15–20 minutes,
or until firm enough to handle.

Shape teaspoonfuls of mixture into small balls, then flatten slightly. Dip into
flour and shake off any excess.

Heat oil in a non-stick frying pan over medium–high heat and fry fritters for
a few minutes on each side until golden. Drain on paper towel and serve
immediately.

SERVES 4

Potato tagine with green vegetables

2 tablespoons butter

1 tablespoon olive oil

3 cloves garlic, crushed

1 teaspoon grated fresh ginger

1 teaspoon ground cumin

1 teaspoon ground cinnamon

1 teaspoon sweet paprika

1 kg small waxy potatoes
(such as Bintje)

8 red shallots or baby
onions, peeled

1 litre vegetable stock

salt and freshly ground
black pepper

500 g mixed green spring
vegetables (shelled broad
beans, peas, sugar snap peas,
snow peas, baby green beans)

½ cup natural yoghurt

fresh mint leaves, to serve

sweet paprika, to serve

Melt butter in a large non-stick frying pan (potatoes and shallots should be able to fit in a single layer). Add oil, garlic, ginger and spices and stir. Add potatoes and shallots and stir to coat vegetables in butter mix. Pour over just enough stock to cover the vegetables, then bring to the boil. Partially cover, reduce heat to very low and simmer for 45 minutes. Check occasionally and add a little extra stock if necessary, but most of the liquid should be absorbed by the potatoes and onions. Season with salt and pepper.

Steam green vegetables for a few minutes.

To serve, pile potatoes and onions on a platter, arrange green vegetables on top and spoon over any cooking juices. Top with a dollop of yoghurt, a scattering of fresh mint leaves and a sprinkling of paprika.

The flavours of this tagine are surprisingly subtle, so match them with the freshest green spring vegetables for maximum effect. Serve with hot chickpeas and warmed flatbread for a delicious meal.

SERVES 4

Punjabi cauliflower & potato curry

250 g waxy potatoes (such as
  Bintje or Nicola)

450 g cauliflower, broken into
  florets

¼ cup vegetable oil

1 teaspoon cumin seeds

1 tablespoon grated fresh ginger

1 teaspoon ground cumin

½ teaspoon ground coriander

½ teaspoon ground turmeric

1 teaspoon curry powder
  (medium or mild)

1 red chilli, deseeded and
  finely sliced

2–3 tablespoons water

salt and freshly ground
  black pepper

1 tablespoon chopped fresh
  coriander

natural yoghurt, to serve

roti or naan bread, to serve

Boil or steam potatoes until just tender. Drain and allow to cool, then cut into 1-cm cubes.

Steam cauliflower for about 5 minutes (or boil for about 3 minutes), then quickly rinse in cold water to stop cooking and drain.

Heat oil in a large non-stick frying pan over medium heat. When oil is hot add cumin seeds and fry for 2–3 minutes. Add cooked cauliflower and fry for a few minutes until it starts to brown. Cover and simmer for 2–3 minutes over low heat.   >

To the pan add potatoes, ginger, cumin, coriander, turmeric, curry powder, chilli and water. (This is a dry curry so there is no sauce – the water is just enough to moisten the mixture so that it doesn't stick while heating.) Stir gently and cook, uncovered, until potatoes are heated through and vegetables are coated in spices.

Stir coriander through the curry at the last minute and serve with yoghurt and warmed roti or naan bread.

SERVES 4–5

Quesadillas

3 spring onions, finely chopped

1 cup chopped fresh coriander

1 cup finely chopped
   flat-leaf parsley

1 red chilli, deseeded and sliced

1 cup grated Swiss or tasty cheese

6 large flour tortillas

1 cup natural yoghurt

GUACAMOLE

1 medium-sized avocado,
   peeled and stoned

1 tablespoon fresh lemon juice

$\frac{1}{4}$ teaspoon chilli paste
   (optional)

salt and freshly ground
   black pepper

To make the guacamole, mash all ingredients together. Set aside.

Mix spring onions, coriander, parsley, chilli and grated cheese in a bowl.

Heat a large non-stick frying pan over medium–high heat (you do not need any oil). Place a tortilla in the hot pan and spread with one-third of the herb and cheese mix, then put another tortilla on top. When tortilla is golden brown (or even a little charred) on the bottom carefully turn over and cook the other side. When browned, slide carefully out of the pan, cover with aluminium foil and place in the oven to keep warm.

Repeat to make two more quesadillas, then cut each into quarters and serve immediately with guacamole and yoghurt on the side.

SERVES 3

Quick veggie curry

2 tablespoons vegetable oil

1 onion, halved and finely sliced

2 tablespoons curry paste
  (mild or medium)

1 × 400-g can chopped tomatoes

300 g broccoli, cut into florets

300 g cauliflower,
  cut into florets

8 baby sweet corn

2 tablespoons chopped
  fresh coriander

2 cups baby spinach leaves,
  stalks removed

natural yoghurt, to serve

naan bread, to serve

Heat oil in a large non-stick saucepan over medium heat. Add onion and sauté for 2–3 minutes until softened. Add curry paste and stir for 1–2 minutes until fragrance is released. Add tomatoes, broccoli, cauliflower and baby corn and bring to the boil. Reduce heat, cover and simmer for 10 minutes.

Remove from heat, add coriander and spinach and stir until just wilted.

Serve immediately in warmed bowls, with yoghurt and warmed naan bread on the side.

SERVES 4

Ratatouille

3 tablespoons olive oil

2 cloves garlic, sliced

½ red onion, sliced

1 small red capsicum, deseeded
and cut into thick slices

2 medium-sized eggplants,
cut into 3-cm cubes

1 × 400-g can crushed tomatoes

½ cup vegetable stock

2 small zucchini, thickly sliced

½ cup pitted kalamata olives

salt and freshly ground
black pepper

chopped flat leaf parsley or
fresh basil, to serve

Heat 1 tablespoon of the oil in a large non-stick frying pan over medium heat. Add garlic and onion and sauté for 3–4 minutes until onion starts to soften. Add red capsicum and fry for a further minute. Add the remaining 2 tablespoons of oil and once it is hot, add the eggplant and sauté until just starting to brown. Add tomatoes and vegetable stock, stir to make sure all vegetables are covered in liquid, reduce heat, cover and simmer for about 20 minutes, stirring occasionally.

Add zucchini and olives to the pan, and cook for a further 15 minutes, stirring occasionally. The eggplant should be very soft, but the zucchini should still be a little firm. The sauce should not be too thin; if it is, increase the heat and cook for a few minutes, uncovered, until it thickens.

Check ratatouille for seasoning (with the vegetable stock and olives you may not need to add any salt).

Serve in warmed bowls, sprinkled with parsley or basil.

🍄 This ratatouille can be served on its own with bread, or with steamed rice or couscous. It also makes a substantial pasta sauce (parmesan cheese goes well with it). The sauce improves in flavour if left in the refrigerator overnight and can be reheated or eaten at room temperature. Cooking time for eggplant can vary depending on how ripe the eggplants are, but it should be very tender and almost falling apart.

SERVES 4 | VEGAN

Red capsicums stuffed
with couscous & spinach

1 cup couscous

1¼ cups boiling water or
   hot vegetable stock

2 tablespoons olive oil

1 tablespoon butter

1 onion, finely chopped

3 tablespoons slivered almonds

1 tablespoon grated lemon zest

1 cup cooked chopped spinach
   (you can use fresh or frozen),
   well drained

½ cup sultanas

1 teaspoon sumac

50 g fetta, cut into small cubes

salt and freshly ground
   black pepper

3 medium-sized red capsicums,
   halved lengthways and
   deseeded

natural yoghurt, to serve

sumac and finely chopped
   flat-leaf parsley, to serve

Preheat oven to 180°C

Place couscous in a small bowl and cover completely with the boiling water
or vegetable stock. Stir, cover and leave for 5 minutes.

Meanwhile, heat oil and butter in a large non-stick frying pan and when
butter is melted add onion and sauté for 3–4 minutes. Add almonds and
lemon zest and sauté for a few minutes until nuts start to brown.

Use a fork to fluff up the couscous, then tip it into the pan with the onion.
Take off the heat and stir through spinach, sultanas, sumac and fetta. >

Season with salt (you may not need it if you have used vegetable stock) and freshly ground pepper.

Spoon mixture into red capsicum halves. Arrange capsicums in a baking dish of suitable size (they should sit fairly close together). Pour 5–10 mm of water into the dish, cover with aluminium foil and bake for 30 minutes. Remove foil and bake for another 5–10 minutes. The capsicums are cooked when they can be easily pierced with a skewer and the top is lightly browned (if you like the edges charred, cook a little longer).

Serve with a small dollop of yoghurt on top, a dusting of sumac and some fresh parsley.

SERVES 3

Roast eggplant with tahini dressing

3 medium-sized eggplants

¼ cup olive oil

1 teaspoon ground cumin

salt and freshly ground
  black pepper

2 tablespoons pine nuts, toasted

DRESSING

2 cloves garlic, crushed

3 tablespoons tahini

2 tablespoons fresh lemon juice

3 tablespoons warm water

salt and freshly ground
  black pepper

Preheat oven to 180°C.

To make tahini dressing, place all ingredients in a small bowl and whisk to blend.

Cut eggplant into rounds about 2 cm thick, brush both sides with olive oil and sprinkle with cumin, salt and freshly ground pepper. Place on a non-stick baking tray and roast in the oven for 25–30 minutes, turning once, until browned on the outside but soft and creamy inside.

To serve, arrange eggplant slices on serving plates, drizzle with tahini dressing and scatter pine nuts on top.

This dish is good served with jasmine or basmati rice, and steamed green vegetables or a leafy green salad.

SERVES 6 | VEGAN

Roast potatoes with cumin seeds

1 kg floury potatoes, quartered
1 tablespoon olive oil
1 tablespoon cumin seeds
salt and freshly ground black pepper
yoghurt mustard sauce (page 243), to serve

Preheat oven to 200°C. Line a baking tray with non-stick baking paper.

Place potatoes in a medium-sized saucepan, cover with boiling water, put on lid and cook for 10–15 minutes until just tender. Drain well, return potatoes to pan, replace lid and shake pan to roughen edges of the potatoes. Add olive oil, cumin seeds, salt and freshly ground pepper, put lid on and shake again to coat potatoes.

Tip potatoes onto baking tray and spread out. Roast in the oven for about 30 minutes, turning once or twice, until golden and crispy.

Serve with yoghurt mustard sauce.

🍄 You can vary the seeds used for this dish, or try fresh sprigs of rosemary, thyme or oregano instead.

SERVES 4 | VEGAN: SERVE WITHOUT YOGHURT MUSTARD SAUCE

Spiced potatoes with baby spinach

12 small waxy potatoes, halved

1 tablespoon vegetable oil

1 teaspoon cumin seeds

1 teaspoon coriander seeds

1 clove garlic, crushed

1 onion, diced

2 cups passata (tomato purée)

1 teaspoon ground coriander

½ teaspoon chilli flakes

2 tablespoons chopped fresh coriander

300 g baby spinach leaves, stalks removed

flatbread, to serve

Steam or boil potatoes for 10–15 minutes until tender.

Heat oil in a non-stick frying pan over medium heat, then add cumin and coriander seeds and fry for 1 minute. Add garlic and onion and cook for a few minutes until onion is soft. Add passata, ground coriander, chilli flakes, fresh coriander and potatoes and stir. Cover and cook for 2–3 minutes until potatoes are heated through. Add spinach and cook, uncovered, until spinach wilts.

Serve immediately with some warmed flatbread to scoop up the vegetables.

SERVES 3–4 | VEGAN

Spinach & ricotta gnocchi

1 tablespoon olive oil

250 g spinach, chopped

200 g ricotta

½ cup plain flour

1 egg, lightly beaten

½ cup freshly grated
  parmesan cheese

salt and freshly ground
  black pepper

fresh basil leaves, to serve

SAUCE

2 tablespoons olive oil

1 onion, finely chopped

6 ripe tomatoes, peeled
  and chopped

1 tablespoon shredded fresh
  basil leaves

salt and freshly ground
  black pepper

To make the tomato basil sauce, heat oil in a medium-sized saucepan over medium heat. Add onion and sauté for 5–6 minutes until softened and golden. Add tomatoes, basil, salt and freshly ground pepper, stir and bring to the boil. Reduce heat, cover and simmer for 10 minutes until reduced and thickened.

To make gnocchi, heat oil in a large saucepan over medium heat, add spinach and sauté until wilted. Drain well and squeeze out any excess water. Place spinach, ricotta, sifted flour, egg, 3 tablespoons of the parmesan, and salt and pepper in a large bowl and mix well. Refrigerate for 30 minutes. >

Roll teaspoonfuls of the gnocchi dough into small balls, until all the mixture is used up.

Cook gnocchi in batches: drop into a large saucepan of salted simmering water and when the gnocchi float to the surface (it only takes a couple of minutes) use a slotted spoon to remove them. Place in warmed bowls, pour over tomato sauce, sprinkle with remaining parmesan and garnish with basil leaves.

🍄 If the ricotta is very fresh and moist, place a piece of clean muslin or a clean tea towel in a sieve or colander over a bowl, place ricotta in and leave to drain until it is firmer.

SERVES 4

Spinach with raisins & pine nuts

¼ cup raisins

3 tablespoons olive oil

2 cloves garlic, sliced

2 spring onions, sliced

500 g baby spinach leaves, stalks removed

¼ cup pine nuts, toasted

freshly ground black pepper

Place raisins in a small bowl, pour over enough boiling water to cover and leave to soak for 10 minutes. Drain.

Heat oil in a large non-stick frying pan, add garlic and spring onions and sauté for 2 minutes. Add well-washed spinach leaves (with water still clinging to them) and cook for a few minutes, turning until they are just wilted.

Add raisins and pine nuts, season with freshly ground pepper, toss and serve immediately.

SERVES 4 | VEGAN

Thai stir-fry
with coconut & coriander

1 stalk lemongrass

2 tablespoons peanut oil

1 long red chilli, thinly sliced

3 spring onions, sliced

1 large carrot, peeled and cut
into matchsticks

250 g snow peas

250 g baby sweet corn

1 red capsicum, deseeded and
cut into long strips

½ cup roasted peanuts

¾ cup coconut milk

salt

½ cup fresh coriander leaves

steamed rice, to serve

Peel outer leaves from the lemongrass, remove bulb, chop stalk finely, then pound in a mortar and pestle.

Heat oil in a large frying pan or wok over high heat. Add chilli, lemongrass, spring onions and vegetables and stir-fry for 1–2 minutes. Add peanuts and stir-fry for another 1–2 minutes (vegetables should still be crisp) then pour in coconut milk and cook until heated through. Check for seasoning and add a little salt to taste if needed.

Stir though coriander leaves and serve immediately, with steamed rice in a separate bowl.

SERVES 4 | VEGAN

Vegetable koftas in curry sauce

600 g potatoes

2 tablespoons finely chopped
  fresh coriander or mint

1 teaspoon ground chilli

salt

1½ teaspoons garam masala

1 egg, beaten

chickpea flour (besan),
  for coating

oil or ghee, for deep-frying

SAUCE

1 large onion, finely chopped

2 tablespoons ghee or oil

4 cloves garlic, finely chopped

1 teaspoon grated fresh ginger

2 tablespoons desiccated coconut

2–4 teaspoons mild Indian
  curry paste

1 cup natural or Greek yoghurt

1 cup water

salt

chopped fresh green chilli
  and coriander, to serve

To make the koftas, steam, boil or bake potatoes in their skins until tender. Allow to cool then peel. Place potato flesh in a bowl and mash until smooth. Mix in chopped coriander or mint, chilli, salt and garam masala. Roll mixture into oval shapes about 6 cm long.

Dip koftas into beaten egg, then dip in chickpea flour to coat thickly. Refrigerate for 2–3 hours.

Heat oil or ghee in a non-stick frying pan and fry koftas about five at a time until golden brown, turning once or twice. Transfer to a serving plate and keep warm.

To make curry sauce, sauté onion in ghee or oil until well browned. Add garlic, ginger, coconut and curry paste and sauté over medium heat for 2–3 minutes, stirring constantly. Pour in yoghurt and water, bring barely to the boil, then reduce heat and simmer for about 8 minutes until sauce is thick and fragrant. Season with salt.

To serve, pour curry sauce over the koftas and sprinkle with chopped chilli and coriander.

SERVES 4–6

Extras

Good vegetarian food is not just about nutrition, it's about variety, flavour and texture, about interesting and unusual combinations. Homemade dips, sauces, dressings and other 'extras' can make a world of difference — and unlike their store-bought cousins, you know just what is in them!

Mix Japanese tamari with Middle Eastern tahini and drizzle it over roast vegetables to create a dish that is nothing like your mother used to make (but many times more delicious). Toss homemade pesto through hot pasta, or add a spoonful to a summery vegetable soup to enhance the flavour. Add your own marinated olives to an antipasto platter or salad. Or try combining a fruity olive oil with good-quality vinegar for an unbeatable salad dressing.

< Avocado & lime salsa (page 222)

Avocado & lime salsa

1 large avocado, peeled, stoned and cut into 1-cm cubes

1 large tomato, cut into 1-cm cubes

1 small red chilli, deseeded and finely sliced

1 tablespoon finely chopped fresh coriander leaves

1 tablespoon olive oil

1 tablespoon fresh lime juice

salt (optional)

Place avocado, tomato, chilli and coriander in a small bowl, pour in olive oil and lime juice and toss gently. Add salt to taste if desired.

MAKES ABOUT 1½ CUPS | VEGAN

Black olive tapenade

1½ cups pitted black olives
1 clove garlic
½ cup capers, rinsed and drained
1 tablespoon fresh lemon juice
freshly ground black pepper
½ cup olive oil

Place all ingredients except oil into a blender or food processor and blend to form a paste. Gradually pour in olive oil and blend until combined (you can make it smooth or leave it a little chunky).

Store in an airtight container in the refrigerator for up to a week.

🍄 Buy good quality olives, even if that means pitting them yourself. Avoid the watery, bland Spanish pitted olives sometimes sold for pizza topping.

MAKES 1½–2 CUPS | VEGAN

Cannellini bean & artichoke dip

1 × 400-g can cannellini beans, drained and rinsed

1 × 170-g jar marinated artichokes, drained

2 tablespoons fresh lemon juice

1 garlic clove, crushed

3 tablespoons extra virgin olive oil

salt and freshly ground black pepper

1 tablespoon finely chopped flat-leaf parsley, to serve

Place beans, artichokes, lemon juice, garlic and oil in a blender or food processor and blend until thick. Check for seasoning (the marinated artichokes can be salty so you may not need extra salt). Store covered in the refrigerator.

To serve, return to room temperature and scatter with flat-leaf parsley.

🍄 Like most dips, this one is better if left in the fridge for a few hours before serving to allow the flavours to develop. If you prefer, you can soak and cook your own cannellini beans using about 200 g of dried beans (see pages 92–93). You can also use other white beans, such as haricot or butter beans.

MAKES 1½ CUPS | VEGAN

Fresh mango & coriander chutney

1 large mango (not quite ripe or slightly green is best)

1 tablespoon chopped fresh coriander leaves

2 tablespoons fresh lime juice

½ red chilli, deseeded and chopped

salt

Cut the mango flesh into small cubes. Place in a bowl with coriander, lime juice, chilli and a little salt. Stir gently to mix.

Cover bowl and chill for at least 30 minutes before serving. This chutney is best eaten within a few hours of being made.

🍄 Spicy but refreshing, this is a terrific chutney to serve with curried vegetables and fragrant rice.

SERVES 4 | VEGAN

Harissa

1 red capsicum, quartered and deseeded

1 teaspoon cumin seeds

1 teaspoon coriander seeds

1 teaspoon caraway seeds

3–4 small hot red chillies, finely sliced

2 cloves garlic, chopped

pinch of salt

4–6 tablespoons olive oil

Preheat oven to 200°C.

Put red capsicum quarters on a non-stick baking tray and roast for 20–25 minutes. Remove from oven, place in a bowl, cover with cling wrap and set aside for 10 minutes (the trapped steam will make it easier to peel off the skins). Remove skins and chop flesh.

Put cumin, coriander and caraway seeds in a dry frying pan and cook over medium–high heat for a few minutes, stirring occasionally, until toasted. Allow to cool, then crush with a mortar and pestle or in a grinder.

Place roasted capsicum, chillies, garlic, salt, crushed seeds and oil in a blender or food processor and blend to a paste.

Spoon paste into a small jar, pour a thin layer of oil on top to help preserve it, then screw on the lid. This will keep for 1–2 weeks in the refrigerator. Pour off oil before using, and always use a clean spoon when removing paste from the jar.

🌶 There are numerous versions of harissa, some made just with chilli and other spices, some with red capsicum and tomato. This spicy paste is eaten in very small amounts (it is hot!) as an accompaniment to dishes such as couscous, and can add zest to a sandwich, hummus or even a vegetable soup. Adjust the chilli quantity in the recipe to suit your taste.

MAKES ABOUT ¾ CUP | VEGAN

Hummus

1 × 400-g can chickpeas, drained and rinsed

½ cup water

juice of 2 lemons

½ cup tahini

2 cloves garlic, crushed

½ teaspoon salt

½ teaspoon cayenne pepper

3 tablespoons olive oil

Place all ingredients in a blender or food processor and blend until thick. Taste and add additional salt or lemon if needed.

Serve at room temperature, with a dusting of cayenne pepper, or with some extra virgin olive oil drizzled on top. Store, covered, in the refrigerator for 3–4 days.

Hummus is high in protein and the tahini gives it an earthy, nutty taste. It is delicious in sandwiches and salads, with felafel, or as a dip with corn chips or vegetable sticks. Make a double batch – it freezes well. I always make it with canned chickpeas as it's so quick, but you can use 1 cup dried chickpeas, soaked and cooked (see pages 92–93).

MAKES 1 CUP | VEGAN

Olives marinated with fresh herbs

¼ cup olive oil

2 cloves garlic, crushed

freshly ground black pepper

1 teaspoon fresh rosemary leaves

1 teaspoon fresh thyme leaves

1 tablespoon grated orange or lemon zest

4 cups mixed olives (e.g. kalamata, manzanilla, jumbo green, etc.)

Place oil in a large bowl, add garlic, pepper, herbs and zest and stir to combine. Add olives and mix well to coat.

Spoon olives and liquid into a sterilised glass jar, seal and store in the refrigerator for at least a week (and up to 2 months). Bring back to room temperature before serving, and always use a clean spoon to remove them from the jar.

These olives are great served with drinks before dinner, as part of an antipasto platter, or just scattered over a simple green salad. If you like some extra spice, add some finely sliced red chilli to the marinade.

MAKES 4 CUPS | VEGAN

Pesto

2 cups torn fresh basil leaves
2 cloves garlic, crushed
3 tablespoons pine nuts, toasted
½ cup extra virgin olive oil
½ cup freshly grated parmesan cheese
salt and freshly ground black pepper

Place basil and garlic in a blender or food processor and blend until well combined. Add pine nuts, then gradually add oil and pulse to form a paste (you can leave it a little chunky, or make a smoother paste if you prefer). Stir in parmesan and season with salt and pepper.

Refrigerate pesto for a few hours before using to allow the flavours to develop.

To store, spoon pesto into an airtight container and pour a little olive oil on top before sealing the lid. It will keep in the refrigerator for a few days.

Stir pesto through pasta for a quick meal, add a dollop to baked potatoes, or use as a spread in sandwiches. You can vary the ingredients – e.g. use rocket and hazelnuts, or coriander and walnuts. If you want to keep the pesto for a few days, it is best to add the parmesan just before serving.

MAKES ABOUT 1 CUP | VEGAN: OMIT PARMESAN CHEESE

Roasted red capsicum & walnut dip

3 large red capsicums, quartered and deseeded

1 cup walnuts, lightly toasted

1 teaspoon sweet paprika

1 tablespoon ground cumin

½ teaspoon ground chilli (optional)

¼ cup olive oil

salt and freshly ground black pepper

Preheat oven to 200°C.

Roast red capsicums on a baking tray for about 20 minutes until softened and slightly charred around the edges. Remove from oven, place in a bowl, cover with cling wrap and set aside for 10 minutes (the trapped steam will make it easier to peel off the skins). Remove skins.

Place roasted capsicum and remaining ingredients in a blender or food processor and blend to form a thick, chunky paste.

Serve this as a dip with vegetable sticks or corn chips, as a spread in a salad sandwich, or as a quick sauce for pasta. This is similar to a Middle Eastern dip known as muhammara; the Middle Eastern version often contains pomegranate molasses, lemon or other ingredients.

MAKES ABOUT 1½ CUPS | VEGAN

Salsa verde with basil

1 cup finely chopped flat-leaf parsley

1 cup finely chopped fresh basil leaves

2 cloves garlic, crushed

1 tablespoon drained capers

1 teaspoon grated lemon zest

1 tablespoon fresh lemon juice

⅓ cup extra virgin olive oil

salt and freshly ground black pepper

Place all ingredients, except oil and salt and pepper, in a bowl. Gradually whisk in oil. Taste and season with salt and pepper if desired.

Cover with cling wrap until ready to use. This salsa will keep in the refrigerator for 2–3 days and improves over time as the flavours develop.

MAKES ABOUT 2 CUPS | VEGAN

Sweet tomato chutney

2 tablespoons virgin olive oil

2 pickling onions, finely sliced

1 clove garlic, finely chopped

½ tablespoon ground coriander

½ teaspoon ground cumin

1.5 kg tomatoes, peeled, deseeded and chopped

½ tablespoon grated fresh ginger

¼ cup soft brown sugar

¼ cup red wine vinegar

salt and freshly ground black pepper

Heat oil in a large saucepan over medium heat and sauté onion for 5 minutes or until softened. Add garlic and cook for 1 minute. Stir in coriander and cumin and cook for 1–2 minutes or until fragrant. Add chopped tomatoes, ginger, sugar and vinegar and stir well. Partially cover and simmer gently for 1–1½ hours, stirring occasionally, until chutney is thick. Season with salt and freshly ground pepper.

When completely cool, pour chutney into a clean airtight jar. Store in the refrigerator.

🌱 This chutney is great with lentil or soy burgers, or with corn fritters. It also makes a special topping for toasted cheese sandwiches.

MAKES ABOUT 1½ CUPS | VEGAN

Tahini sauce

½ cup tahini
2 tablespoons tamari or soy sauce
juice of 1 lemon
about ½ cup water

Combine tahini, soy sauce and lemon juice in a bowl, slowly adding water and stirring until you have a smooth sauce. Use less water to make a thicker sauce.

Store in the refrigerator, but return to room temperature before serving.

Tahini sauce is amazingly versatile: try it drizzled over felafel or salad in a wrap, on roasted vegetables (especially eggplant, zucchini and capsicum), with couscous or rice, or even as a salad dressing.

MAKES 1 CUP | VEGAN

Tamari-roasted nuts & seeds

400 g mixed shelled nuts (e.g. almonds, hazelnuts, cashews, peanuts)

50 g sunflower seeds

50 g pumpkin seeds (pepitas)

100 ml tamari

1 tablespoon sugar

¼ teaspoon dried chilli seeds

Preheat oven to 180°C.

Spread nuts and sunflower and pumpkin seeds over a non-stick baking tray and roast for 10 minutes, shaking the tray once or twice to turn them.

Mix tamari with sugar and chilli in a medium-sized bowl. Add roasted nuts and seeds and stir to coat. Tip nut mixture back onto the baking tray, spread out and roast for a further 5–10 minutes, until dry and lightly toasted (check frequently to make sure they don't burn). Remove from oven and leave to cool on the tray.

Store nuts in an airtight jar.

🍄 This mix is a great nibble to have with drinks, but can also be added to salads or scattered over steamed rice or couscous.

MAKES ABOUT 3 CUPS | VEGAN

Vinaigrette

1 clove garlic, crushed

½ teaspoon Dijon mustard

salt and freshly ground black pepper

2 tablespoons white wine vinegar

3 tablespoons olive oil

Put the garlic, mustard and a good pinch of salt in a small bowl and mix until well combined. Add vinegar and oil and whisk together. Add some freshly ground pepper to taste.

It is best to make this dressing just before serving.

How you like your vinaigrette is very much a personal taste – some people prefer a sharper flavour, others more subtle, so adjust the quantities accordingly. Use a balsamic vinegar for a darker dressing with a smoother flavour, or experiment with different types of oil.

MAKES ABOUT ⅓ CUP | VEGAN

Yoghurt mustard sauce

1 cup natural yoghurt
1 tablespoon Dijon mustard

Stir yoghurt and mustard together until smooth.

Refrigerate until needed. This sauce will keep, covered, in the refrigerator for 2–3 days.

🥄 Yoghurt sauce is an easy, quick, nutritious sauce that is ideal with roasted or steamed vegetables, in a lentil burger or as a dip. For a grainy mustard sauce, substitute the Dijon mustard for French grainy mustard. For a lime yoghurt sauce, substitute the mustard for 1 tablespoon lime juice and a teaspoon of finely grated lime zest. And for a peppery wasabie yoghurt sauce, substitute the mustard for wasabi paste.

MAKES 1 CUP

Zaatar

3 tablespoons sesame seeds
3 tablespoons dried thyme
1 heaped tablespoon ground sumac
salt

Put the sesame seeds into a frying pan over high heat and dry-fry them for a few minutes, shaking the pan occasionally, until toasted (watch them carefully as they can burn). Tip seeds into a small bowl and allow to cool.

Add thyme and sumac to cooled sesame seeds, add a small pinch of salt and mix well.

Store in an airtight jar in a cool place or in the refrigerator for up to 6 weeks.

Zaatar is a mix typical of Middle Eastern food, and is wonderful sprinkled over yoghurt or over warmed flatbread that has been brushed with a little virgin olive oil.

MAKES ABOUT ⅔ CUP | VEGAN

Glossary

BALSAMIC VINEGAR is a dark, mellow, aged vinegar with a complex yet subtle flavour. The true balsamic is made in Italy from Trebbiano grapes and aged for at least 12 years in wooden barrels. It can be used with oil in a dressing, or by itself on salads, vegetables and even fruit.

BUCKWHEAT is a nutritious high-protein grain, better known in Russia, Japan and China than in the West. It is used in flour and in Japanese soba noodles. It does not contain any wheat so is suitable for those on gluten-free diets.

BURGHUL (also known as bulgar, bulgur and cracked wheat) is the coarsely ground inner bran of the wheat grain. It is similar to couscous, but has a harder nutty texture. It is common in Middle Eastern cooking, for example in tabbouleh or served as a pilaf or like rice to soak up sauces.

COUSCOUS, although it looks like a grain itself, is a product made from wheat. Steamed or soaked, it is widely used in Middle Eastern recipes. There are various sized grains available, but in Australia the fine grain is the most common. Couscous has a bland flavour and is a practical alternative to rice and pasta.

DU PUY LENTILS are a small green variety of lentil, traditionally grown in France, and generally considered the finest of the lentil varieties. Like other lentils they are high in protein and fibre. This type of lentil is now grown in Australia.

GARAM MASALA is an aromatic blend of ground spices used to season curries and to sprinkle over finished dishes. Its chief spices are coriander, cumin, pepper, cloves, cardamom, cinnamon and nutmeg, though it can contain many others. You can mix your own blend.

GHEE is clarified butter. It can be heated to a high temperature without burning as it does not contain any milk solids. It is useful for cooking Indian-style food, especially if you like to cook your own spices, but you can substitute butter or oil if necessary. Ghee is available in supermarkets and Asian food stores.

HALOUMI is a salty, semi-soft cheese, originally from Cyprus, and used in Greek and Middle Eastern cooking. It is stored in brine and has a high melting point, making it suitable for grilling and frying. It can be eaten fresh but is usually served cooked.

KECAP MANIS is an Indonesian soy sauce that is dark, thick and sweetened with caramelised palm sugar. It adds a glossy rich colour and sweet–salty flavour as a seasoning or garnish. It is available in supermarkets and Asian food stores.

LEMONGRASS is a long fibrous stalk that exudes a distinctive lemon aroma when cut. It is used in South-east Asian cooking (especially Thai), often ground into a paste with other ingredients. The tough outer layers need to be removed and the inner layers pounded or very thinly sliced before use. If the whole stalk is used during cooking it should be removed before serving as it is too tough to be edible.

MISO is a fermented soybean and grain purée that comes in various colours (the darker the colour, the longer the fermentation and the stronger the flavour). White miso is the lightest and sweetest in flavour. It is heavily salted but highly nutritious (containing protein, vitamin B12 and minerals) and is said to aid digestion. It is widely used in Japanese cooking, especially in stocks and soups.

PALM SUGAR is a brown sugar derived from the sap of the sago palm or that of various other palm trees. It varies from pale to dark; the darker the colour, the stronger the flavour. You can use soft brown sugar as a substitute.

PANEER is a mild, rennet-free Indian cottage cheese that retains its shape when cooked. It is available at Asian food stores and specialist food suppliers. Baked ricotta (page 34) can be used as a substitute if necessary.

RAS EL HANOUT is an exotic Moroccan spice mix (the name means 'house blend'), which combines spices and aromatics such as nutmeg, coriander, cardamom, chilli, fennel and ginger. You can make your own blend, roasting and crushing the spices. Sprinkle over vegetables before roasting, or add to soups and vegetable tagines.

RICE WINE VINEGAR (also known as rice vinegar) is made from fermented rice or rice wine. It is commonly used in Chinese, Japanese and Korean cooking. It is milder and not as acidic as some Western-style vinegars, being more like **balsamic vinegar**.

RISONI (also known as orzo) is a small rice-shaped pasta. It cooks quickly and can be used in place of rice, polenta or more traditional pasta – as a side dish, in a salad or as a main course with a sauce. A couple of tablespoons of risoni can be added to a vegetable soup to make it more filling.

SESAME OIL is a cold-pressed oil with a rich dark colour and distinct flavour. It is used only in small quantities, in dressings and stir-frys.

SOBA NOODLES are thin Japanese noodles made from 'soba' or buckwheat and wheat, and can be served hot or cold. For those on a gluten-free diet there are some varieties available that are made from **buckwheat** only. They are usually available from specialist wholefood suppliers and Japanese food stores.

SUMAC is a sour-tasting spice commonly used in Middle Eastern cooking, particularly in salads.

TAHINI is a thick, oily paste with an earthy flavour, made from ground sesame seeds. There are two varieties; the paler version, which has a more refined flavour, is made from hulled sesame seeds. Tahini is a nutritious addition to vegetarian cooking and can be used in dips, sauces and dressings. It is widely used in Middle Eastern cuisine, in dishes such as hummus.

TAMARI is a Japanese sauce made from fermented soybeans, and is richer and darker in flavour than Chinese-style soy sauce. It is made without wheat so it is gluten-free and can be substituted for traditional soy.

TOFU (also known as beancurd) is a white curd made from soybeans. It contains a high level of protein and the amino acid lysine, so it can play an important part in vegan, vegetarian and semi-vegetarian diets. Tofu is similar in many ways to a soft curd cheese. It is a staple food in China and Japan, and is widely used in other Asian cuisines. It is usually sold fresh, soaking in water, or vacuum packed, and is also available deep-fried. It is now readily available at supermarkets as well as specialist food stores.

UDON NOODLES are thick, white wheat noodles with a bland flavour, traditionally used in Japanese cooking. They are similar to spaghetti but with a softer texture and are typically served in a soupy broth. They are available fresh or dried at supermarkets and Asian food stores.

Conversions

Celsius	Fahrenheit
160°C	320°F
170°C	340°F
180°C	360°F
200°C	390°F
220°C	430°F

SIZES

Centimetres	Inches
1 cm	²⁄₅ in
2 cm	⁴⁄₅ in
2.5 cm	1 in
3 cm	1¹⁄₅ in
4 cm	1³⁄₅ in
5 cm	2 in
6 cm	2²⁄₅ in
8 cm	3 in
12 cm	5 in
18 cm	7 in
28 cm	11 in
35 cm	14 in

WEIGHTS

Grams	Ounces
50 g	2 oz
75 g	2½ oz
100 g	3½ oz
120 g	4 oz
150 g	5 oz
200 g	7 oz
225 g	8 oz
250 g	9 oz
300 g	10½ oz
350 g	12 oz
400 g	14 oz
500 g	16 oz (1 lb)
600 g	1⅓ lb
800 g	1¾ lb
1 kg	2 lb

LIQUIDS

Millilitres	Fluid ounces
100 ml	3 fl oz
200 ml	7 fl oz
400 ml	13½ fl oz
600 ml	20 fl oz (1 pint)

Index

PENGUIN BOOKS

Published by the Penguin Group
Penguin Group (Australia)
250 Camberwell Road, Camberwell, Victoria 3124, Australia
(a division of Pearson Australia Group Pty Ltd)

New York   Toronto   London   Dublin   New Dehli   Auckland   Johannesburg

Penguin Books Ltd, Registered Offices: 80 Strand, London, WC2R 0RL, England

First published by Penguin Group (Australia), 2008

10 9 8 7 6 5 4 3 2

Text and photographs copyright © Penguin Group (Australia), 2008

The moral right of the author has been asserted

Many thanks go to Freedom Furniture in South Yarra, Matchbox in Armadale and
Dinosaur Designs in South Yarra, who provided a selection of the lovely props.
Thanks also to Paul Nelson for all his help, the perfect coffees and the magic table.

Cover and text design by Claire Tice © Penguin Group (Australia)
Photographs by Julie Renouf
Food styling by Lee Blaylock
Typeset by Sunset Digital, Brisbane
Scanning and separations by Splitting Image Pty Ltd, Clayton, Victoria
Printed in China by Everbest Printing Co. Ltd

National Library of Australia
Cataloguing-in-Publication data:

Barca, Margaret
Vegetarian bible.
978 0 14 300855 2 (pbk.)
Vegetarian cookery.

641.5636

penguin.com.au